Beneath
the
Grandstands

To Shannon
Best Wishes

Ray Crump

Beneath the Grandstands
By Ray Crump as told to Ray Crump Jr.
Copyright © 1993 by Ray Crump

ISBN 0-9637884-0-X

Printed in the United States of America

Published by: Crump Publishing Co., Inc.
910 South Third Street
Minneapolis, MN 55415
First Edition

Foreword

Ray Crump is a man unlike ordinary men. I say this not because he is my father, nor because I am writing his life story.

I've seen the look in people's eyes when he tells them a story. Stories I have heard a hundred times before, but yet I continue to listen.

I see his emotions come through in his hands as he speaks of someone he once knew or only briefly met. His actions are as sincere as people's reactions to him.

Although many people do not know him by name, many have heard stories of him. Either gaining their knowledge by stopping by his store/museum, or perhaps remembering a blurb from some distant newspaper of their past.

He is somehow seen as special through the events in which he participated. Or at least that is what people have told me.

Regardless of whether or not you have heard of Ray Crump, he is worth remembering. Herein lies his life story.

Ray Crump Jr.

Table of Contents

Chapter 1

The Early Years

I was born in our nation's capital, Washington D.C. in 1936, and by geographic association, I followed the Senators.

When I was twelve, a friend of mine, Ronnie R. Stant, worked as a visiting clubhouse bat boy at Clark Griffith Stadium. He invited me to go to the ball park with him, and I cheerfully agreed. When I went to the stadium, I was fortunate enough to get a job in the visiting locker room as an errand boy.

My job was just as it sounds. I would act as a gopher for the players. I would complete various tasks for the players. For all my running, I was paid the grand sum of fifty cents per game plus tips from the ball players. Out of this stipend, it cost me thirty-four cents for round-trip carfare. Sixty-eight percent of my income went to transportation costs.

But money was never a large concern of mine. The highest pay I ever received as a bat boy was $2.50 per game, but I was working for a professional ball team. I ran home, extremely excited, and told my father about my new job. I informed him that I was going to be an errand boy at Griffith Stadium and would eventually become a bat boy.

My dad chuckled as he often did when I told him my goals. He said, "There's no way you can do that job. They have men who do that job, they just call them bat boys. Because they have to travel all over the country, little kids like you can't travel all over the country. You couldn't get that type of job." My father was wrong, I did get the job. And it was just the beginning.

My life as a bat boy was very time consuming as was the life of an errand boy. I participated in many different jobs when I worked for the Washington Senators. I ran down to local stores or restaurants to pick up sandwiches for the players and I ran back and forth to the cooler for sodas or beers.

The other clubhouse boys and I shined approximately seventy pairs of shoes every day and cleaned the locker room. To make matters worse, those were the days of real grass. Thus, on rainy days, the cleats were filled with a thick infield mud. After the team's train came into Washington from a road trip, we would go to the stadium at night and unpack all their equipment bags to prepare them for the next game.

There were many things to do besides the actual baseball game.

On night games, the players usually entered the locker room between 2:30 and 5:00 p.m. When they arrived, we were prepared to do their bidding. We would get them anything they needed to get ready for the game. In addition, we helped them with "club business." In other words, we would get them balls to sign and help them answer their mail. Closer to workout time, our duty was to carry the bats and other necessary equipment from the locker room to the dugout. As the players took batting practice, we would shag balls in the outfield. This was the most enjoyable part of the job, mingling with the "Gods of the diamond." We also would play catch with the ball players to warm up their arms (and to wear out ours).

I soon discovered that baseball is a series of hierarchy and progressions. It's not entirely different from the private (non-baseball) sector. Players usually have to start in A-Ball and move their way to AA, and finally to the "auto club" before they make it to the major leagues.

Meanwhile, a clubhouse worker goes from errand boy to visiting bat boy, followed by ball boy, home team bat boy, assistant clubhouse manager, visiting clubhouse manager, and finally home clubhouse manager. Of course, people occasionally bypass some levels.

In 1951, while I was the visiting bat boy, Cleveland came to town. Prankster Red Kress, a coach for the Indians, and their manager, Al Lopez, played a joke on me.

After a game, another bat boy and I were walking down the street with baseballs from the stadium. Red was waiting for a cab on the corner, and offered us a ride. When we started down Florida Avenue toward Kress, the balls came loose and started rolling down the street. We scrambled frantically to pick up the baseballs. When we stopped one ball, another would start to roll and then another. It was similar to a skit one might see on "I Love Lucy." I was scared to death of getting in trouble for losing the valuable pearls.

Later, at the stadium, Al and Red started kidding us, "Red did you miss any baseballs today?"

Red answers, "Yeah, we lost about seven of them."

Both had a completely serious face until slowly they began to crack up together.

Lopez, since we're speaking of him, was one of the best managers ever because he could get a player to hate him and play for him, or like him and play for him. Having players hate and/or like ball players, is very difficult to accomplish, but Lopez was successful at bringing out their best.

Al Lopez was just a super guy. He was a very nice man who would go out of his way to help others. I'll give you an example of his kindness. My car broke down in the off season.

Lopez saw I was having problems and he pushed my car with his Lincoln until it started.

The next year, I became the home team's ball boy at Griffith Stadium. My job was to sit down the foul line and gather balls that were sliced in my direction, or I would sit in the dugout and give balls to the home plate umpire upon request.

Finally, I became the Washington Senators bat boy and held that job until 1955. I worked under the wing of Fred Baxter, the Senators' equipment manager, and he taught me the trade. Eventually I became the visitor's clubhouse man.

While still a bat boy, I gave my father a ticket to a ball game. He told me later that he had sat up in the stands and pointed me out to a person sitting next to him.

"See that bat boy out there, that's my son." My father pointed me out proudly to his neighbor in the stands.

The man, equally proud, said to my father, "See that ball boy? That's my son."

Complimentary tickets were allotted to various stadium personnel for family and/or friends. Calvin Griffith was very generous throughout his baseball ownership. I received a total of six tickets for each game. Often, as in every game, my list of friends was high. People tend to be more friendly when you have something free to give away.

5

The great ball players during my Senators days were: Roy Sievers, Harmon Killebrew, Jackie Jensen, Mickey Vernon, Jim Busby, Camilo Pascual, Chuck Stobbs, Jim Lemon, and Bob Allison. Some coaches at the time were Ellis Clary, Heinie Manush, George Myatt, and Joe Haynes (a former major leaguer and Calvin's brother-in-law). The managers in Washington while I was there were Bucky Harris and Chuck Dressen.

I was nicknamed "Ninety-Seven" by Heinie Manush as a bat boy for Washington. He derived this name from a ball that was put out by the Rawlings Sporting Goods Company called, "Ball-Hawk 97." When a ball was hit down the line, Manush and later the other ballplayers would shout, "Get that ball, Ninety-seven."

The number ninety-seven was actually the first number retired by Calvin Griffith. He said that he didn't want anyone else to wear "Ole Ninety-seven." Thus, he ordered the number to be off limits. It was a great moment for me. After my number was retired, the Twins retired numbers of great players like Harmon Killebrew's number three, Rod Carew's number twenty-nine, and Tony Oliva's number six.

My sons, Andy and Ray, who are now in their mid-twenties, often made road trips with the team in spring training. To see them running out in the field always made me happy. Not because of a potential for them to be ballplayers, but rather they reminded me of my experiences as a youth.

I guess you could say I was reliving my childhood vicariously through them. I wanted them to have the same great and memorable childhood that I was fortunate enough to experience. They really enjoyed the club atmosphere. Their mother tells me that little Ray made comments about growing up and doing my jobs. He also said he felt important when he was with me, which made her reply, "What am I, chopped liver?"

Andy enjoyed fishing with various players, especially Ron Davis and Al Williams. Andy went fishing with Ron Davis when they experienced difficulties with the engine. Ron told Andy to fiddle with some wires on the motor.

"Why don't you do it?" Andy asked.

Ron held out his hands and said, "Do you know how much these things are worth? I'm not touching that engine."

Whenever I would go on a road trip with the team, Carol, my wife, would tell the boys that I was working. Andy was watching the game on television and saw me in the dugout. Andy screamed, "Look Mom! Daddy's not working, he's just sitting there."

* * *

My father had a race horse named Captain Cress. The horse was racing at Charleston Racetrack in West Virginia. I constantly told the players about my father's horse. Spec Shea, Mickey Grasso, Chuck Stobbs, and manager Bucky Harris all went to the track several times to watch my dad's horse. The horse raced five times and came in dead last every time. Each time, the players bet on the horse. And each time, the players complained to me when it lost.

We had an off day coming up and I told the players that Captain Cress was running that day. Of course, they were reluctant to get "bit" again, but agreed to give the horse one last chance. The horse was a thirty to one long shot, but the horse was blessed by a miracle and won the race.

As my father strolled to the circle to have his picture taken with the horse, he smiled from ear to ear. Normally, the jockey poses with the horse, but my father was so excited that he took over. Suddenly, the horse dropped dead of a heart attack and was hauled away in the back of a pickup truck. From that day forward, all the players called me "Ninety-seven," except Bucky Harris, who called me "Captain Cress."

Bucky Harris took me to breakfast at the Lamp Post restaurant in New York. As we were sitting eating, a woman crashed her car through the wall of the restaurant and skidded right next to our table. Bucky didn't flinch a muscle. The rest of the diner patrons dived on the floor and under tables (myself included). Bucky sat calmly with his cup of coffee in hand and turned to the woman who was still shaken up. "That is some way to enter New York City."

Another memorable event in my life as a bat boy occurred when "The Golden Boy," Jackie Jensen, was traded to the Boston Red Sox. He was a great guy, and I was sorry to see him leave. Yet, he didn't forget me when he joined the Sox. I'll never forget one of my first trips to Boston as a bat boy. Jackie picked me up in a big Cadillac. Very few ballplayers had a Cadillac and his was even a convertible. He picked me up and showed me the city of Boston. He was a first-class guy.

The players were constantly joking around and playing tricks on one another and me. I remember one trick that they got me on, and I used it several times myself in the following years. I'm sure if I would have taken the time to think about what they asked me to do, I would have discovered the lunacy of their request. However, I was so eager to do a good job, I hurried to complete my assignment.

I was told I needed a key to the pitcher's mound. I ran to a player and asked him for the key to the mound. He said,

"Sorry, I just had it. Check with the trainer."

Upon entering the training room, "Sorry, I gave it to the manager."

I ran to the manager's office, he said, "I had it a minute ago, I gave it to the pitching coach."

This went on and on until I finally figured out what they were doing. The guys all laughed at my search of the elusive and nonexistent key to the pitcher's mound.

Howard Fox joined the Washington Senators as traveling secretary in the fifties. He asked me if I could drive a little truck on part of a barnstorming road trip. In barnstorming trips, two professional teams would travel to small cities who rarely were afforded the opportunity to watch major league baseball. During these days, players would dress in hotels and head out to the fields. Often, the fields were simply grassy areas with a canopy like you might see at a funeral, used for dugouts.

I had my driver's license for about six months, and reluctantly agreed to drive the small Hertz rental truck. The Reds' equipment manager and I were to drive Cincinnati's and Washington's equipment to the train station. When I went to pick up the truck, all that they had left was the large multi-geared semi-trucks. I explained to them that I couldn't drive a manual transmission truck and asked to have a Hertz employee drive it to the hotel. I thought once we were at the hotel, the Reds' equipment manager could drive it. Someone did, but soon after it was parked outside the hotel a police officer told us to move it.

I told the policeman that I couldn't drive the truck, but I would get the man who could. The officer wasn't interested in any of this; he just wanted the truck moved. I frantically searched throughout the hotel and finally located the missing driver. The equipment manager promptly notified me that he was unable to drive at all, and he didn't even have a license!

The cop, unmoved by this revelation, said sternly, "You have to move it."

I figured out how to work the stick and started driving toward Columbia, South Carolina with loud, popping, engine sounds. The truck jumped up and down like a bronco, but we made it to the hotel. We stayed at the brand new Holiday Inn, one of the first in the country. A couple of players and umpires were also staying in the hotel.

I was tired from the trip and nearly passed out on the bed from exhaustion upon entrance to my room.

There was a loud annoying knock on the door. The bell captain informed me that I had to move the truck, since it was disrupting the traffic flow.

Now at this point, I knew that I could barely drive the truck, but I had to move it. The bell captain was behind the truck offering directions as it slowly moved in reverse. Everything was well until I heard and felt a loud crash. I had backed directly into the overhang in front of the new hotel.

The next day, the team arrived and Jim Lemon was on the bus. "Oh my God," exclaimed Lemon as he saw the damage to the roof. "Ray has arrived."

He was joking, but was very surprised when he discovered he had hit the nail on the head.

The next day, I had to drive to Augusta, Georgia, where they have the Augusta Open and the Masters' Golf Tournament. When I arrived, they had a circular driveway with an overhang, just like the one I had just smashed. I had learned my lesson the first time and I realized the truck should be moved from the hazardous area. I began to back up the semi when a significant motorcade pulled up behind me.

Upon later investigation, I discovered the convoy occupants were the secret service and President Dwight D. Eisenhower. I was blocking the path of the most powerful man in the world.

Finally, I was able to get the truck out of the way so the chief executive could get through my blockade.

The next day in the Augusta newspaper, on the front page, it said, "Trucker Holds up President."

Years later, I was driving down Constitutional Avenue in Washington, D.C. with a great friend of mine, Andy Payne. When I stopped at a light in my convertible, a large limousine pulled up beside me and the window rolled down. Inside was then Vice-President Richard M. Nixon. He looked at me, grinned, and said, "Hey, Ray wanna drag?"

My friend went wild. I knew Nixon because he was a big baseball fan. I think that some politicians go to ball games for merely political reasons, but President Nixon was different. He called the front office and asked for the inning. If there were a couple innings left, he would rush to watch the end of the game. Nixon's love of baseball afforded me the opportunity to meet him.

Each clubhouse in both American and National Leagues used to have what was known as "a swindle sheet." On this sheet, players would write down what snacks or sandwiches they had while in the locker room. When the series was over, the players would pay the clubhouse men for the items they consumed and tip us. Vice-President Nixon, would take a beer and put in on the swindle sheet under a player's name. He shouted across the room, "Hey, Ray put this one under Yogi

[Berra]."

When John Fitzgerald Kennedy ran against Nixon for president, I wanted Kennedy to win. Andy Payne thought I was completely nuts. He said, "Here's a guy who is running for president, knows you by your first name, wanted to drag race you, and then you want the other guy to win." It was funny, on Election Day, I went over to this guy's house and he said he figured it out. He said to his parents, "The only reason he's here is to run his mouth. The only reason he wants Kennedy to win is because he's Catholic and Kennedy's Catholic. But he's still nuts."

When I was a visiting clubhouse man in Washington, I did a lot of work on players' bats and gloves. I often re-strung players gloves when they started to come apart. This was before the athletic companies gave dozens of gloves to players upon request. More importantly, one of the things I've done is the well known practice of "corking" them. The corking process involves drilling out the bottom of the bat and removing the wood. After the wood is removed, cork is placed in the middle of the "sweet-spot." Then rosin would be placed on the bat and set on fire for about thirty seconds. The fire would make the bat appear as though it had never been altered or manipulated.

The cork itself would give the ball a little extra push when hit well. The extra few feet could mean the difference between a long out and a home run. It made a big difference for a couple of players whose bats I enhanced. Two of them are now members of the Baseball Hall of Fame in Cooperstown, New York.

When the players came to town in the old days, they arrived by train. In addition, they didn't have individual equipment bags. Rather, they used several large trunks, which contained medical equipment, bats, helmets, and equipment. Each equipment trunk contained room for the uniforms, gloves, and other items of six players. Each of the six players had a tray of equipment in the trunk. When the train came to town, I would bring the trunks to the clubhouse and put a tray on top of each locker. Since the trays contained the name and number of each player, they knew exactly where their locker was positioned.

They used trunks to carry equipment because they could be more easily protected from thieves. A player like Mickey Mantle was a prime candidate since he was immensely popular. Once, he lost a glove and offered a reward of three gloves and no questions to the person that returned his mitt. Ballplayers are notorious for their superstition, and he was convinced that he needed this particular glove.

He had worked on it with Johnson's Baby Oil and had it formed to his exact specifications. Eventually, I found the glove and sent it to him. He had thrown it over the locker and it had wedged between the locker and the wall. He was ecstatic when I told him I had found his prized possession. But, I never did get the three gloves.

Diligent workmanship was very common with ballplayers and their special relationship with their equipment. Besides spreading baby oil all over their gloves, some players left them in a sauna all night. They hoped that it would make the glove softer. I suppose this could have been the early development of the phrase, "Soft hands."

Also, players used to "Bone" their bats. I went down to a meat market in Orlando and purchased a ham bone. I left it outside for several weeks and let the sun bake it. When it was time to leave for Minnesota, I skinned the rest of the meat off the bone and attached it to a table. Players could then rub their bats on it to smooth out the wood grain. Soon, clubhouses throughout the league all had ham bones. Players could rub their bats in cities all over the United States.

Players were always doctoring their bats, through corking or other more superstitious means. Umpires and other players knew it, but the officials rarely enforced the rules. They needed a manager or player to complain about an odd piece of equipment to take action. Generally, players didn't complain about each other, since both sides had teammates who bent the rules. Of course, Billy Martin was famous for pointing a finger at players. The pine tar episode with George Brett and the disqualification and then reinstatement of his home run in 1983, remains the most memorable rule infraction in the history of professional baseball.

I think that the days of enhancing bats was much more prevalent in my Washington days than in Minnesota. People did everything they could to give themselves a competitive edge. In addition, many of today's players probably don't know how to doctor their bats. In general, I think the interest in baseball and intensity in which the game is played has waned since then.

In 1961, I became the equipment manager for the Minnesota Twins when they moved from the nation's capital to a farm community in a small town known as Bloomington, Minnesota.

Fred Baxter remained in Washington to work for the

"New Senators." (A new expansion team that moved into Washington.) I was 25 and the youngest equipment manager in baseball.

The job of equipment manager involved many different activities. In a brief nutshell, I had to order bats, uniforms, equipment, upkeep the locker room, take care of the player's every whim, and take charge of the staff.

I tried to make our new dressing room a "home away from home." The players could relax and prepare themselves to play baseball. I called Koval Appliance to get a television for the clubhouse. I afforded him the opportunity to "loan" the television to the new professional ballclub.

Every spring training, a meeting was held to determine who would be wearing the uniform of the Minnesota Twins. A professional baseball player's uniform was custom made to the exact specifications and dimensions of the athlete. When we had this meeting, Calvin Griffith, Howard Fox, a representative from the sporting goods company, and I would discuss the uniforms. Since the uniforms are specially designed, we had to order them in advance. Howard would give his opinion on whom was going to make the trip up North, and we would make a list.

A pitcher received two complete road and home

uniforms. Infielders, outfielders and catchers each received three full outfits, since they played more and would put more wear and tear on their jerseys and pants.

After the meeting was over, the sales representative and I would go over the list again and make whatever changes were necessary. Occasionally, Howard and I disagreed about the possibility of a player making the trip up North. In these instances, I would trust my instincts and order the uniform despite what Howard had said. Normally, I was correct, but even if I was wrong, it was easy to take the number back off the jersey. This typifies the day in the life of an equipment manager.

When the players ordered bats, they would tell me the size and weight of the lumber. During the year, I would order a couple dozen bats for each hitter at the beginning of the season and more if they needed them. Before the designated hitter rule was imposed as a permanent rule in 1975, pitchers would get one dozen bats for the entire season. I only ordered two bats per season for Dean Chance, since he rarely even touched the ball. His lifetime batting average was .066, and even less during his time in Minnesota.

My family toured the Louisville Slugger plant in Kentucky. By coincidence, Dean Chance's order for a dozen bats was being made. I said this had to be a mistake, since we only ordered two bats for him. We would have ordered only one, but we were worried he might lose one.

Normally, the team equipment manager would call directly to Louisville Slugger to place the order. Fox wanted to parlay his order into a free gift at the expense of the club. Howard always wanted me to give him the order sheet, because the company also made golf clubs. Howard was an ardent golfer and placed the orders to receive free golf clubs.

I still received many other perks as a member of the organization. Every month during the baseball season, Gene DaCosee of Wilson Sporting Goods Company would send me a dozen golf balls. I didn't play golf at the time, so I gave the balls to my brother Burton, who lived in Virginia. The Twins had a big golf tournament at Southview Country Club in Mendota Heights. I was playing in the tournament, when I saw that a top executive from Wilson was playing in the next group. I am, without a doubt, the world's worst golfer. They were right behind me, and I was hitting golf balls everywhere. They were landing in the lake, on the beach, in the woods, and everywhere else the balls could land. I turned to Gene and says, "Now, you see where all those balls you sent me went."

The Twins were receiving many bills from a detective

agency in Orlando hired by Bob Willis, who was working for the Orlando Twins in Florida. Sherry Robertson, Calvin Griffith's brother (Calvin's original name was Robertson, he changed it to Griffith when adopted by his uncle, Clark Griffith) and farm director at the time, was on the phone back to Minnesota. He was asked why they were getting all the bills. Willis said that he hired the detective agency because Clyde, who was the longtime grounds keeper at Tinker Field, was stealing baseballs.

Robertson had an immediate solution to the problem. He got off the phone and told Joe Haynes to call the detective agency and tell them that we didn't need them anymore. Following that, Haynes was told to have Willis go out to the field and tell Clyde to stop taking baseballs. The detective bills stopped.

In 1967, when Sam Mele was managing the team, we played two exhibition games with the Boston Red Sox in San Juan, Puerto Rico. Before we left, I was concerned because we were told that each player needed a passport. I said to Fox, "These players forget their gloves, how are they supposed to remember a passport? We could get the passports and hand them to each player as they go through customs. Or better yet, show them a team photo." Of course, the customs agents wouldn't go for that. They didn't care who you were, if you didn't have a passport you couldn't get into the country. Fox held all the passports for the players and handed them to each person as he passed through customs and collected them as they left.

We played in San Juan Saturday and Sunday we had a game in Ponce, which was a small town up in the mountains. We had to take two little airplanes, which only seated 16-18 people each. While we were in San Juan, we didn't sell out the entire stadium. I was talking to the promoter, who spoke only fragmented English. He told me that he had mortgaged his house to guarantee each team the $35,000 required. In addition, if Sunday's game was sold out, he would have to give each team $10,000. The man thought that the stadium would be more than half full, but expected a sell out the next day in Ponce. He was very concerned about the possibility of losing his house.

When we arrived in Ponce the next day, it was raining. They didn't have a tarp to cover the field, and it was in a terrible condition. They had some old men with coffee cups who slowly removed water from the field and poured it into a pan they held. It didn't help, the field was still in miserable shape. The day before, we were the visiting team, and Sunday Boston was the visiting team. So Sam Mele and I talked about it, and Sam said that the field was in rough shape and he wanted to call it off. I agreed, but I felt sorry for the promoter. I tried to reach Howard Fox, because he couldn't make it to the exhibition due to a golf outing in San Juan. After talking with Calvin, Howard would make decisions about rather or not to call off these ball games. I couldn't get a hold of Howard, but I told the promoter that we could delay the game until 3:00 p.m. He was very grateful for the delay, since it gave him an opportunity to recoup his losses. In addition, since we had a plane to catch, no inning could start after 4:45 p.m. I wrote this agreement out on the back of a brown paper sack, and called Calvin to confirm the deal. Everything was set and we started playing the game.

It got to be a quarter to five, and I was in the locker room packing our bags. Jim Wiesner, the visiting club house manager, said that Sam was talking to the umpire who wouldn't let the game end. The umpire threatened us with a forfeit if we left. However, since it was an exhibition, we really didn't care if we were given a loss. I ran out to the dugout, and the umpire exclaimed, "Ray, we can't stop the game."

I knew we had to catch the plane, so I walked toward the field and started waving in the players. Everyone in the stadium started booing. I told the umpire the agreement I had with the promoter, and we had a plane to catch.

"It was his responsibility," I said. "to tell the people that it would be a shortened game."

"Did he inform the crowd?" The umpire was trying to figure out what to do.

"I can't be sure, because I don't speak Spanish." The umpire wasn't amused by my comment.

I led the rest of the players away from the field. Johnny Sain, the Twins pitching coach, went crazy. He said, "I can't believe that a clubhouse guy can call a ball game."

We got on the plane from San Juan to Miami and Calvin came down the aisle and said, "Raymond, ya did a real good job. You made both of our clubs an extra $10,000. I wanna thank ya."

I was sitting with Sam Mele, who had a couple of drinks. He looked toward Calvin with glazed eyes. He slurred, "Jesus Christ, why don't you give him a raise if he made you some money."

Later, during the regular season, I was in the club house and was not paying any attention to the game when the phone rang. I picked up the phone and I heard Calvin's voice on the line. He was all excited and said, "Raymond! Raymond! Tell Sam to protest the game."

I didn't know what was going on, but I ran down the tunnel and into the dugout. Sam was out on the field arguing with the umpire. I didn't want the players to know that Calvin wanted the game protested, so I walked toward him on the field. I went up next to him and said, "Calvin says protest the game." My mission was complete and I walked back to the dugout.

He turned to me and said, "Ray, what did you say?"

I turned back to him and shouted, "I said, protest the game." Johnny Sain went nuts again. He threw his towel up in the air and said, "Jesus Christ, he called one in Ponce and he's protesting one here in Minnesota."

A hair care product called Vitalis, by Bristol-Myers, often was able to find its way in various press photos.

I was in charge of distribution to all the clubhouse managers in the league. I made a deal with the company in which I would receive $100 for getting the product in the paper. I cut a second deal with the UPI photographer and would give him $25 every time he took a picture of the player and the bottle.

It was really kind of funny, I would place bottles in many different players locker rooms, especially when they had a good game. I even put one in Harmon Killebrew's locker, which was amusing since he was losing hair at the time.

* * *

I wanted to provide the players with an alternative to their regular post-game dinner. I called Rose Totino, who owned a local pizza restaurant and told her I wanted to buy pizzas wholesale. She said that I didn't have to buy them, because she would give them to the team. The food was used as an incentive to make the players perform to their potential during a time without million dollar contracts.

During some ball games, I used to make the pizza in the seventh inning when the team was winning. It was funny, sometimes I would have to take the pizzas out of the oven when the team was losing. Then, they would retake the lead and I would put them back in the oven. It would go back and forth; some of those pizzas got cooked pretty well.

Rose wanted to get Jim Kaat to do a commercial for her. Kaat told her his fee, which was much more than she was willing to pay. She said that she might as well give me the money. She put me up in a chef's hat, and took some pictures for the newspaper. Soon after that, a check arrived at my house for around $700. I sent the check back to her because she had given us free pizzas. She called and said that I was the only person in her lifetime whom she wanted to give money, but refused to take it.

On a related story, I've done a few speeches for different groups. Of course, I didn't require as high of an honorarium as some players. I gave a speech at some convention in Minnesota. I wasn't exactly their first choice. During my speech I said, "You called Harmon Killebrew, but he wanted a thousand dollars. Then you called Bob Allison, but he wanted four hundred dollars." I pointed to my dinner and stated, "You got me for a chicken dinner." The audience laughed and I enjoyed my chicken.

Chapter 2

Calvin Griffith

Calvin invited the clubhouse workers and the ground crew out to dinner during spring training. He allowed us to choose the restaurant and we selected Freddie's Steak House in Orlando. The steak house was a popular hangout of the players, coaches and staff. When we arrived at Freddie's, Howard Fox, his wife, Dr. McKenzie, and Dr. Harvey O'Phelan unexpectedly walked into the lobby and Calvin had a funny look on his face. Calvin hadn't invited Howard and his entourage, but rather they had overheard someone talking about the free dinner. We sat in the middle of the restaurant, and they sat at a table adjacent to ours.

Fox said, "Hey boss, why don't you sit with us?"

Calvin retorted, "I'm not sitting there" and he sat by my wife, Carol, and myself.

A short time later, the server came by and Howard ordered drinks for everyone at his table. Calvin became very upset at this.

He said, "He has the audacity to order drinks before us. And I'm paying for this whole dinner."

The next day, Calvin called Howard into the office and

said, "I don't want you ever to do that again. When I want you to come to dinner with me, I will invite you. Don't ever pull a stunt like that again. You know what? I didn't even want you there."

Fox had a stunned look on his face, but Calvin was still very upset that Fox would invite himself and others for a free dinner without asking permission. Rather than causing a huge scene at the restaurant, Calvin decided to handle it privately.

When Roy Smalley was getting married, Carol and I planned on attending until my oldest son became sick. Carol called off the babysitter, but said that I should still go to the wedding and reception. The reception was held at the Calhoun Terrace Club in Minneapolis. I went to the wedding alone. Calvin Griffith, Howard Fox and his wife Yvonne also attended. A cash bar was set up outside the reception hall. I took their drink orders and returned with drinks for the four of us.

Howard asked, "How much did they charge you?"

Calvin thought it was strange to be charged for drinks at a reception. "Charge? You mean their charging for drinks here?"

Fox responded, "Yes, they have a cash bar set up outside. And they're serving champagne later." Fox always knew when he might receive something free. Calvin began to retrieve his wallet and Fox subtly glanced away.

I stopped him. "No, Mr. Griffith. I've got this."

He looked very surprised. "Raymond let me tell you something. You are the first person in this organization who bought me a drink, and didn't plan on putting it on their expense account."

As we were walking up to the buffet line, Calvin whispered to me, "Raymond, don't eat much. We'll go out to eat later."

After dinner, our group decided to leave the reception. Calvin flung his arms through the air and said "Well, I'm really tired. I think I'll go to bed."

Howard was somewhat shocked since it was still early. "Boss, don't you want to go out and get a couple of drinks somewhere?"

"Nah, I think I'll go home." Calvin responded without looking at Howard.

Howard and his wife left and we continued to walk to our cars.

Calvin said, "Raymond, I'll meet you on the parking lot of the Steak and Ale in Bloomington." When we got in the restaurant he said, "You know, I just wanted to get away from

Howard Fox."

We had a nice dinner, and I could tell he appreciated me buying him a drink. It was amazing how little of a gesture it was on my part and how much of a difference it made to him.

Equipment managers are not under a pension plan like the trainers. I was trying to get all the equipment managers together to talk to their teams. If the teams voted and more than fifty percent of players voted positively, then the clubhouse people would be placed on the pension plan. I went to Calvin and showed him the letter that I had written before sending it to the other equipment managers. A guy that worked for the White Sox named Roland Hemond suggested that Calvin fire me for trying to start a union.

I honestly wasn't starting a union. Since I was working sixteen or eighteen hours a day for nine months every year and missing time with my family, I felt I deserved some kind of financial security. Trainers were involved in the plan even though they didn't arrive until two o'clock and they left immediately after the game ended.

Calvin agreed with me and I was placed on the pension plan. I was the only equipment manager in the history of baseball to ever receive a guaranteed contract, and I will have a small pension waiting for me when I retire for which I am very thankful.

Calvin was always fair to me, which is a contradiction to the way he had been portrayed in the press. He was always seen as a miser, but was very generous to the people close to him. Whenever there was a Minneapolis Chamber of Commerce "Welcome Home Celebration," or other team function, Calvin would always introduce me. Mentioning the equipment manager was a rare event within the league.

Occasionally, when the Twins had a day off, a player would come in to work out. Therefore, I had to go to the ball park and wait for him. This took away one of the few times during the baseball season that I could spend quality time with my wife and young sons. Calvin disagreed with this solo workout. He would tell me to lock the door and go home. He felt I needed a day off also. Not many owners today would do that. Many equipment managers never even see the owner today, and the owner doesn't always know who handles the clubhouse. Calvin, on the other hand, always considered his workers part of his family. I consider him alongside my father.

Calvin had a real heart. Once, we went into Falconers Cleaners on Lake Street in Minneapolis. It was a very hot day and Calvin was impressed with the employees that had to suffer

33

through the heat to clean our uniforms. He said he wanted to do something for them, and he followed through with his words. He gave all the employees and their families complimentary tickets for a ball game. Ever since that hot and humid summer day, for at least fifteen years, Calvin had "Falconers Cleaners Day at the Met." He would give them three to five hundred tickets per game for the employees and their families.

Calvin's generous gestures were not limited to this occasion, despite what the local press said about him. There were several occasions when he would call me up to his office as he was looking out the window.

"See those kids out there," Calvin said pointing to a few kids asking people for extra tickets. "They don't have any money for the game. Go let them in, but don't tell them I had anything to do with it."

I followed his instructions and led them through the Twins offices, into the stadium, and the kids were very excited and grateful.

We were driving by the corner of 90th and Portland when Calvin saw a neighborhood field in really poor condition. When we got back to the ball park, Calvin called Dick Ericson and directed him to get the ground crew together. Then, he instructed them to go to the field and fix it up. So a professional grounds crew, without any fan fair or press releases, went to a city field and repaired it for the children to enjoy.

Calvin gave my father an American League pass, which granted him free admission for any American League game. My father treasured that pass and was constantly going to watch ball games. Before he passed away, he gave the pass to my brother Burton. He wanted to continue that baseball tradition, and my brother was as big of a baseball fan as my father. Burton manages an American Legion team in Virginia, and has won the championship a couple of times. He went to every spring training when I worked with the club except one. When my sister, Norma, was dying, he skipped Florida to be with her. Even now, while I am no longer involved with baseball, he still goes down South every spring training.

There were rumors floating around that a few members of the Oak Ridge Boys and Conway Twitty were interested in buying the Minnesota Twins Baseball Organization. Patrick Reusse, who wrote for the *St. Paul Dispatch* at the time, called Calvin in an attempt to solidify these rumors.

He asked Calvin, "Do you know Conway Twitty?"

Calvin smiled and replied, "No, I don't. I don't know as many people as Ray Crump."

It was rather amusing and Reusse wrote about it in one of his columns.

I never got along with the pitcher Mike Marshall when he was with the club in the late 1970s. Apparently he told a player that he would like to see me out of the clubhouse.

The player laughed and shook his head. "You have a better chance of getting rid of Thelma Haynes [Calvin's sister] than you do of Ray Crump."

This episode showed the close relationship between Calvin and me.

Calvin Griffith was criticized for much of his time in Minnesota for his thriftiness. In reality, he was a very generous man, who took care of people he cared about. Calvin treated thousands of people well from his shoe repairer to his employees and family. After Dave Boswell's career was over for the Twins, Detroit and Baltimore, he encountered some financial difficulties. Calvin gave him a job "bird-dogging," and paid him much more than the normal rate. A "bird-dogger" goes to high school games to watch and report on certain players, since a scout cannot attend all the games. Calvin also loaned Harmon Killebrew over a hundred thousand dollars. He never received anything in return, except a letter from a bankruptcy court. Calvin has given hundreds of thousands of dollars to the

Williams' Fund at the University of Minnesota. These generous actions are rarely mentioned in the press, unless they need to fill some space.

Calvin still regularly treats former employees to dinners and parties. It has been over nine years since he sold the ball club in 1984. I went to three of these occasions in 1992 alone. It's rare that you hear about this side of his generosity. While he owned the ball club, he would have a Christmas party every year. Calvin would instruct all the executives to serve the regular employees. He used to give thousands of dollars in Christmas bonuses, not to mention raises. Contrast that to Carl Pohlad's Christmas bonus of Twins Highlight video tapes, which epitomizes the new ownership. From my experience, I see Mr. Griffith amongst the greatest and most generous people I've ever met.

Every year, when I was with the Twins, I drove my family and the Twins station wagon down to Florida for spring training. One year, as I walked into the office Calvin said, "Did ya get any tickets."

He knew that I was notorious for speeding.

"Yes," I told him. "I got one."

He laughed, "Well, don't worry about it. Just put it on your expense account and I'll pay it."

After the season, I handed my receipts to Ossie Bluege, who played for the Senators for many years and now worked in the front office. He threw the receipts up into the air and said, "I'm not paying for any speeding tickets."

I said, "Yes you are, because as soon as the World Series is over, I'm going to call Calvin collect. And he'll tell you to send me a check." When I left the office, he told Jack Alexander, who worked with him, to send me a check.

Ossie said, "He'll call Calvin and he'll tell us to send Ray a check. Plus, he'll call collect and it'll cost us more money."

Major League Baseball held a players' strike during spring training one year. Calvin approached me in the locker room. "I want to know how much the strike is costing you and I want you to get that figure to me today."

I figured out everything from clubhouse dues to tips and gave the figure to Calvin.

He looked at the paper and said, "Raymond, tomorrow go to the accounting office and there will be a check for you."

I guarantee that I am one of the only clubhouse men in baseball who was still paid when there was a strike.

There was a precision sky diving team who used to land

on the pitcher's mound during some spring training games. Once they landed, they would hand a game ball to whomever was throwing out the first pitch. One sky diver got caught up in a heavy wind and hit the fence in center field at Tinker Field. Calvin Griffith automatically said, "We'll take care of his medical expenses."

Howard Fox was all upset at what took place and told Calvin, "We can't take care of his expenses. If we take care of his expenses, then we're liable."

Undaunted by what Fox had said, Calvin interjected "Find out what his expenses are and donate that amount to the sky diving team."

The Twins were under no responsibility at all, since the team asked for permission to land on the field. It was a great thrill for them. None of this mattered to Calvin who wanted to do what he thought was right.

In 1977, Elvis Presley appeared in Orlando. When I arrived at Tinker Field, Calvin showed me a newspaper article promoting his appearance. He said, "Raymond, I would like to go to that concert."

I was baffled by his statement. Calvin did not seem like the type of person that would want to go to a rock n' roll show.

Not only did he mention the concert, but he told me about that concert a few months in advance.

About a week before the concert, I reminded Calvin of the show and he said that he would have to check his schedule. I didn't want to disturb him further, so I went to the show without him.

When Elvis appeared at the concert hall, he didn't like the seating arrangements. It was shown "In the round," which means seats were behind the band. He complained to Colonel Parker. He said, "Look, I do not want to play to these people with them just looking at my back. I want you to give all their money back."

The concert had been sold out for quite some time, so there wasn't any money available to give the concert members. Elvis eventually performed his show with the people sitting behind him.

The next day, Howard Fox came and told me that Calvin was very upset that I went to the concert without him. I went in and said, "Mr. Griffith, I took it that you didn't want to go to the concert. When I asked you about it this week, you said you had to look at your appointments. So, I figured you didn't want to go."

He was really kind of upset, but I assured him that we

would go to the concert when Elvis appeared in Minnesota.

I got in touch with Elvis' people to get tickets for the concert. Jackie Kahane, who was the opening comedian before Elvis' show, brought over the tickets to the ball park. He gave me the tickets, which I placed in my back pocket. Then, I arranged to pick up Calvin after the day game to go to the show. As I looked for my tickets later in the day, I was unable to find them. I was really worried, since Calvin was counting on me to take him to the concert. I thought he wouldn't believe what had happened and would be disappointed again.

I phoned the St. Paul Civic Center. I figured since the tickets were from Elvis, they would know the location of the seats. When the phone was answered, I received a recording that stated the offices were closed for the day. I started to get more concerned. It was six o'clock at the time, I needed to go home and change, and then I was supposed to pick Calvin up at seven. I called Elvis' hotel and left a message for Joe Esposito, his road manager, to call me at the stadium. When he returned my call, I told him the story and asked him if he had the seat numbers. I was afraid that he wouldn't believe that I had lost the tickets, but I lacked an alternative. I thought he might think that I was trying to acquire more tickets, since they were very difficult to obtain. As I was talking to him on the phone, I could hear Elvis talking to someone in the background. Meanwhile, I was perusing the room frantically. Finally, I saw the tickets on top of the toilet of the manager's office. I still have no idea how they landed in such an unusual location.

"Wait a minute, Joe," I said. "I found the tickets."

He said, "Great, where did you find them?"

"On top of the commode." He started laughing profusely and Elvis asked him what was so funny.

I could hear him answer. "Ray is flushing your tickets down the commode."

After I got off the phone with Joe, I went home and changed for the concert. Carol was already dressed when I arrived. A few minutes later, we were off to pick up Calvin. We were very late when we got into the auditorium because of the problem with the tickets and also because the ball game ran late. All the parking spaces were filled and I was forced to park on the grass next to the Civic Center. Calvin said, "Raymond you can't park here."

I said, "I don't have a choice, it'll be fine."

When we went into the concert hall, Calvin wanted a drink. I told him that they didn't have drinks, but I could probably get him a beer. I looked for ten minutes, but couldn't find any stands selling liquor. When I returned to the seats with beer in hand, I saw a great big sign saying "Liquor." It was the first time they had put liquor into the arena for an event, Calvin was right.

There was an announcement over the loudspeaker: "Ladies and gentleman, we have a special guest in the audience this evening. Calvin Griffith, owner of the Minnesota Twins, is attending the show."

Everyone in the audience began to applaud. After that, Elvis came out and performed a fabulous concert. Calvin really enjoyed it. He tapped his foot nonstop throughout the show to the music and smiled throughout the show. When we left the Civic Center, we discovered that our car had not been towed. In fact, we had started a trend. About two hundred cars parked on the grass. Calvin chuckled, "Only Raymond Crump could get away with that."

When we went back to Calvin's condominium, he said, "That was really great. It was a really great show. Just great."

I thought he was referring to the concert, "You really liked Elvis?" Calvin smiled, "Oh yeah. He put on a good show, but that's not what I'm talking about."

"What are you talking about?" Carol jumped into the conversation.

"They clapped for me," he said with a grin. "If we had

been back at the Met, everyone would have booed me."

Calvin was on a plane heading back to Minnesota from Orlando when he started talking to the man next to him, who introduced himself as Bill Anderson. Calvin said, "I'm Calvin Griffith owner of the Minnesota Twins."

Anderson said, "Oh yeah, I have a very good friend that works for the Twins."

Calvin asked him who he knew.

"Ray Crump," he responded.

Calvin then said, "Oh yeah. Well, why are you going to Minnesota?"

He looked at Calvin and said, "Well, I am heading to Peabody's Bar in Inner Grove Heights."

Calvin then got off the plane and told me he had met a friend of mine.

I asked, "Who did you meet?"

"I met a bartender who works at . . ." he said pulling out a piece of paper. "Peabody's in Inner Grove Heights. His name was Bill Anderson."

I thought it was hilarious, and I rushed home to tell Carol. Calvin wasn't aware that he was talking to the country music singer.

* * *

Calvin called me in the locker room and said, "Let me ask you something. Do you have the key to Gene Mauch's apartment?" I said that I did and Calvin said, "Good, I want to go over and see his apartment."

We arrived at the apartment complex, which happened to be owned by Sid Hartman. Calvin said, "It's a strange thing. I just found out that Mauch was living in this apartment building."

At the time, Mauch's contract stated that the Twins would pay his rent. Calvin was just shocked that Mauch was staying in the penthouse of the complex. He said, "When I was looking at apartments, I couldn't even afford to stay in this place. And now, I'm paying for the whole god damned thing."

He was literally paying for everything, from the toilet tissue to the light bulbs.

I had an abscessed tooth, which was causing me a tremendous amount of pain and problems. I am afraid to death of the dentist, so I kept putting it off. Finally, Calvin convinced me to go to the team dentist, Gary Jacobson. When I went to his office, he told me that he had to pull my two wisdom teeth. Obviously, my fear of dentists and pain increased exponentially. Still, the dentist convinced me that the extraction was for my own good. After Gary pulled the teeth, I went home and went immediately to the bedroom and fell sleep. At twenty minutes after eleven, the phone rang and Carol answered.

Calvin said, "Carol, this is Calvin. How is Ray?"

My wife responded, "He's fine, I don't think he's in that much pain. Do you want to talk to him?"

She went to get me on the phone.

"Hello, Mr. Griffith." I said this slowly in an attempt to mask the pain. My cheeks were swollen with a disgusting combination of blood, cotton balls, and inflamed tissue. I looked like a chipmunk with a mouth full of nuts.

Calvin sounded very concerned. It was as though he could sense the pain I was feeling before he called. "I went to bed at ten, but I couldn't sleep. I was worried about how you were feeling, so I decided to call. I'm sorry for calling so late and I hope I didn't wake you up. I just wanted to make sure you were all right."

"Everything is fine." I tried to put Calvin at ease. "You just get some sleep."

This is typical of Calvin. He didn't talk about business at all. He was merely concerned about my condition.

Every year, toward the end of the season, the Twins hold

a "Fan Appreciation Night." Today all the prizes are given by corporations, rather then the team purchasing the promotional items. When Calvin owned the ball club, he would buy all the gifts using the ball club's money. Every year Calvin would give a car as the grand prize. A Twins employee went to pick up the drawing tickets for the automobile.

When the winning number was drawn for the car, two people came down to the field and claimed the prize. Calvin assumed that there was a printing error and that two identical numbers were printed. He never suspected fraud. His only choice was to buy another car so that each person would be a winner. Eddie Weller was cleaning up Metropolitan Stadium after the contest and found a couple large rolls of tickets in the outfield bleachers. A printer, or someone who worked in the business, printed a second batch of tickets for the contest. The fraud cost Calvin two cars.

When Calvin was looking for someone to buy the team, Donald Trump offered him fifty million dollars. According to baseball regulations, an owner has to entertain offers in the city in which the team played. In other leagues, the NHL for example, a team can move without league approval. If Calvin had the same options, he would have been able to sell the team for much more money. The deal with Trump fell through when a local businessman, Carl Pohlad, bought the club. A deal he later regretted. The only other regret Calvin had was not hiring former Twins' Earl Battey and Lenny Green as coaches.

But, his biggest regret was selling the club to Pohlad. He said, "I sure wish I could have sold it to Harvey Ratner and Marv Wolfenson, who own the Minnesota Timberwolves basketball team. They are more honorable people than Carl Pohlad. Carl Pohlad is nothing but a liar."

Not that we should feel sorry for Calvin Griffith. He does have a great deal of money, and he is aware of that fact. He took Carol and me, along with some of our friends out to dinner in Florida. I felt bad because, I didn't think it was necessary for him to pay for our friends. He said, "Don't worry about it. I'm not sure, but I think that I may have more money than you."

Unfortunately, Calvin now avoids the Metrodome and his true love of baseball for fear of running into Pohlad or Howard Fox.

On September 28, 1978, Calvin gave a speech to the Lion's Club in Waseca, Minnesota. In the speech, he mentioned Jerry Terrell who lived in Waseca. Terrell was a utility player for the Twins from 1973 to 1977. He was a success story in that he made the club on a try-out camp. He wasn't heavily recruited from high school, he just showed up and made the team.

Calvin said in his speech, "Now here's a guy who doesn't even belong in the major leagues, but proved hard work can pay off."

In the same speech, Calvin was asked why he moved the team from Washington. He answered, "I moved the team because the blacks go to wrestling matches."

His thoughts caused a huge uproar at the time, but they were more motivated by demographics than racial slurs. At the time, few blacks went to ball games. Thus, rather than a racial attack, it was merely a business move. Granted, he should have worded his comments much differently. Yet, Calvin was known for speaking his mind, which often got him in hot water. What Calvin said was nothing compared to comments made by Marge Schott, the Reds' owner, in 1992. Those statements would have caused an even larger outcry today. There was a newspaper reporter in the audience that misinterpreted Calvin's words and the whole thing blew up and an outburst ensued.

At the time, the Twins had an "executive committee," that was chaired by Howard Fox. They used Fox as the chairperson. If the post had been occupied by Calvin's son,

Clark, or Thelma Haynes' son, Bruce, it would have amounted to nepotism. This executive council felt that they would lose many season ticket holders because of Calvin's comments. Howard Fox, felt that Calvin should be ousted as president. Fox graciously suggested that he would take over as president.

I went up to Calvin and told him what was taking place. He calmly said, "Raymond, I want you just to sit here." Then he left the office and went to the conference room.

He walked down to where the meeting was taking place, opened the door. He stated, "There is no longer an executive committee. And I want you all to go back to your desks and go to work."

He came back to me and said, "That takes care of that." Soon after, the fallout over his comments ended.

Charles Daniels would chauffeur the late Clark Griffith around. When Griffith was dying he told his adopted son and nephew, Calvin, to make sure that Daniels had a job. After Clark Griffith passed away in 1955, Calvin gave him a job in the concessions department. Calvin brought Daniels with him to Minnesota, which was fortunate since only a few people made the trip up North. Daniels didn't have any money at the time, so Calvin gave him a personal loan, free of interest so he could buy a house. This further dispels the myth of Calvin being cheap. He wasn't under any legal obligation to hire this man. In addition, because Daniels is African-American, this contrasts the view of Calvin as a racist.

A topic of interest, which Calvin always had to answer to involved one of his most cherished players. Whenever someone asked Rod Carew's status with the ball club. Calvin said, "Rod Carew signed a contract for $170,000. And he was a damn fool to sign for that amount. Regardless, he has a contract with the ball club that he is obligated to fulfill."

In the end, Calvin couldn't afford to keep Rod any longer. He went to the Angels and many consider this to be the start of Calvin's fall from grace in Minnesota. Only those who truly understood the game and the money at stake supported Calvin during this time. Calvin was using his personal money, rather than using the capital of a corporation. Thus, it was more than a tax right-off for Calvin when the team lost money.

Calvin's biggest fault was that he was too much of a baseball fan. He loved the game with all his heart. If someone screwed up, he wasn't above openly criticizing the performance. He would always speak his mind, unlike the people involved with baseball today. A player cost the Twins a game by dropping an easy fly ball. After the game, a fan asked him about the error.

He answered in all sincerity, "It was terrible. You could have caught that ball in your back pocket. And these guys are supposed to be professionals."

It's like holding a Pepsi in your hands and saying "You know this isn't very good." You can't take a product that you own and are trying to sell, and then knock the product. Calvin was just too much of a fan for his own good. If you're an owner of baseball, you cannot be honest with the public at all times, which is why people like Carl Pohlad are successful.

Calvin authorized a book to be written about him, in which he gave the writer, Jon Kerr, a list of people he wanted interviewed. The list contained Harmon Killebrew, "that boy that came from Washington with me, Ray Crump," and others. The writer didn't contact many of these people. The book was written and sold a few thousand copies, but it didn't turn out the way Calvin would have liked. Calvin then said that if he ever had another book written, he would make sure it was done his way. Including a whole chapter on "that no good son-of-a-bitch Carl Pohlad."

My main reason for writing a section on Calvin Griffith is to try and clarify the many misconceptions of the man. If there had been more people like him, the business of baseball would not be in the mess it is in today. Television contracts can only help pay a portion of the outrageous salaries. For most teams, twenty-five percent of their income is derived from television. With CBS losing millions of dollars, the amount fans pay will increase. In the end, the fans will be the ones hurt by turning the national pastime into the national corporation.

Chapter 3

The Players

In 1961, we were playing a game in Cleveland and I received an anonymous call stating that a player would be shot if the Twins won the second game of the doubleheader. Security and the police were called to the stadium. We held a meeting to discuss the phone call. Cookie Lavagetto told the players, "Ray received a phone call that said if we win this game, one of our guys will be shot."

Jim Lemon looked unconcerned. He stood up and asked, "Well, did they say who they were going to shoot?"

Jim was a happy-go-lucky guy who wasn't concerned unless he was in the guns sights. A lot of extra security was rushed to the stadium and tensions were pretty high in the clubhouse. Threats are fairly common in professional sports, but rarely do they come true. Thankfully, in this case, the threat was not carried out to any degree. Perhaps the extra security scared the assailant away. But I'll never forget Lemon's question.

In 1968, Lemon became the manager of the Washington Senators. He also owned a small "mom and pop" store in College Park, Maryland next to the University, which he ran in the off season. Though we didn't work together, we were still close friends. I was driving from Annandale, Virginia, which is near Arlington, to Orlando for spring training and I brought a bunch of Twins pennants and stickers with me. I decided to go out of my way before I headed South. College Park was only 15 miles from Arlington. I stopped by Jim's store at night, which was called "The Store." When Lemon arrived for business the next morning, he discovered Twins logos plastered all over his building.

In January, 1975, Harmon Killebrew came over to my house and told me that he was thinking about going to Kansas City. His wonderful career was over in Minnesota, and Calvin had offered him a job as a minor league manager at Tacoma or a player/coach with the Twins. Killebrew thought he could still hit and didn't want to take advantage of either of Calvin's offers. He called the general manager of the Royals from my house and took the job.

Whitey Herzog managed half the season and didn't plan on playing Killebrew every game. Harmon finished with only 312 at bats, fourteen home runs, and a dismal batting average of .199. It was a tragic end to a great baseball career. References about it are still made today. George Brett was quoted as saying that he didn't want to end his career like Harmon Killebrew. If Killebrew would have taken the job in Tacoma he would have definitely been an eventual manager of the Minnesota Twins.

Calvin Griffith didn't like the players wearing the long stirrup socks. We had special socks made up, and Calvin wanted me to make sure that we threw out the old socks. We were in Winter Haven for spring training on a Saturday before Easter and I was sitting in the dugout. Howard Fox came down to the field, because Calvin wanted to see me. He was upset that the players were still wearing the long stirrups, which didn't show the white sock between the stirrup and the shoes.

"What's the deal Raymond?" Calvin asked. "I thought you were going to buy the socks so they couldn't stretch them."

"I did, but the players went out and bought their own socks." He instructed me to remove all the socks from their lockers when we returned to Orlando.

After we got back to Tinker Field, I removed the stirrups as I unpacked their equipment bags. I knew the players would be upset at the apparent theft of their personal items, but I was just following the owner's order. I walked over to the blackboard, which was primarily used to tell players the workout schedules and departing times for road trips. I scribbled on the board, "The Easter Bunny has stolen your socks."

When the players came into work, they weren't happy about the missing socks. Bob Allison, who was the player's representative at the time, was told by Jim Perry that I had taken the socks. Allison said, "You have no right to go into my locker or anyone else's and take out our personal items."

"You know, all the socks are over at Calvin's hotel room." I said looking Allison in the eye. "Why don't you go over and tell him you would like the socks back."

He became infuriated. His face turned bright red and his eyes burnt into me. "Calvin doesn't have any right to tell you to take our personal belongings."

He shouted continuously and said he was going to tell Calvin this and that. We had the argument by the equipment room and the players in the locker room could easily hear our loud discussion. It was probably the first argument that Allison and I had since he was with the ball club.

I went over to the telephone and called Calvin's room. I told Allison, "You're full of crap. You've got a lot of bull. You won't tell Calvin anything that you say you will. If you are going to say anything, tell him now." I held out the phone for him.

Allison's eyes bulged out of his head even further. He took the phone and slammed it down. He grabbed me and threw me against the wall. I admit that I was a little intimidated. After all, he was a big guy at 6'3" and 205 lbs.

I said, "You're gutless, Allison! You're gutless! I used to have a lot of respect for you, but now I don't!"

"This is how much I care about the respect you have for me!" Allison pinched his thumb and forefinger together.

I started my barrage again. "You know, you're horse shit! You're gutless! You tell the players you are going to talk to Calvin, but you're scared to death of him!"

Meanwhile, he still had me pinned against the wall. Finally some players came to my rescue and pulled us apart. I didn't even talk to the son-of-a-bitch for the next week. I didn't want to have anything to do with him. I just did my job and let him do his. Years later, we solved this sock controversy by adding a "TC" to the stirrup.

My brother Burton came down for his usual spring training excursion. We went out for drinks at a local bar. The waitress came over to us with a tray of drinks, which we hadn't ordered. I asked her who the drinks were from and she pointed to a table occupied by Bob Allison and Ron Kline.

"Take these drinks back," I said, "And tell him to stick

them up his ass." The waitress looked confused, but did as I had asked.

Allison brought the drinks back to our table and passed them around. "Hi," he said. "I'm Bob Allison, where ya from?" He acted like a complete phony that night.

Eventually, we put our differences behind and became friends again. Unfortunately, Allison is in rough shape now. He suffers from the nervous affliction, ataxia. I will always remember him in his vibrant days, though we were not always on the same side of the fence.

I only had one argument with Rod Carew in all the years he played for the Twins. Bruce Haynes, Calvin's sister's son, wanted Carew to autograph a bat for the Minneapolis Children's Hospital. He told Bruce that he wouldn't sign the bat. Rodney was having contractual arguments with the ball club, and wasn't interested in helping the club's public relations. I asked Bruce to give me the bat. I planned on waiting for Carew to calm down, then present him with the bat to sign.

The team came back from a road trip, and I thought enough time had passed. I went over to Carew and asked him to sign the bat.

He pushed the bat away. "That's the bat that Bruce

Haynes wanted me to sign and I won't sign it."

Rod, like many greats, was known to have mood swings. Most of the time he was extremely nice, but he was unreasonable when upset. These swings could be caused by any number of factors from problems at home to a hitting slump.

"Rod, you told the people at the hospital that you would sign the bat. They have already advertised it in an auction. If you don't sign it, you're horse-shit. You are not signing it for the Twins, you're doing it for the children. You're just embarrassing yourself, not the ball club."

He stared aimlessly at the wall in front of him. "Well I'm not signing it."

I took the bat and threw it into my locker, which was at least 25 feet away, and I walked away. My son, Ray Jr., was in the locker room at the time and Rod asked him to go get the bat. My son was only about ten at the time, and didn't comprehend that Rod and I were mad at one another. He signed it and handed it back to my son, and said "Your dad sure was hot." That was probably the only argument I had with him in the many years he was in Minnesota.

Carew was a great guy but as I said, he could be moody. We had a day game and everyone on the team had left except Rod. I was tired also, but I saw him packing his bag.

"What are you doing?"

He looked very serious. "I'm going home."

"What do you mean?"

"I'm quitting the game," he said without changing his expression. "I'm quitting and going home."

I said, "You don't want to quit the game."

He ignored my statement and asked me to drive him to the airport.

I couldn't believe what I had heard. "You've got to be crazy to think I'll drive you to the airport. Let me tell you something. Someone will go to Calvin and they'll say, 'Mr. Griffith, Rod has jumped the club and Ray drove him to the airport.' You're nuts if you think I'll drive you there."

We sat and talked about it, and eventually he decided to stay with the club. I'm not sure why he was upset on that occasion, I think he felt unappreciated by the club. If the Hall of Fame ballplayer had left, it would have been a terrible loss for baseball.

In 1991, the Minnesota Twins had a "Tony Oliva Day at the Metrodome." It was a special day for everyone as the number six was being retired. Rod Carew came into Minnesota to give a speech for Oliva, and he watched a couple of innings in Mr. Pohlad's private box. He then suggested to his wife,

Marilyn, that they stop by my store next to the stadium to say "Hello." She didn't think it would be proper for them to leave, since the Twins flew them into the Twin Cities.

The next inning, Rod asked again about going to see me. Again, Marilyn didn't think it was appropriate. Rod was adamant and kept telling Marilyn that he wanted to leave, but she protested. Finally, after a couple more innings, he had enough. "Marilyn, I'm going to see Ray with or without you."

Rod and Marilyn came over to the store a few minutes after their conversation. Rod wore a suit and dark glasses in a futile attempt to disguise himself. I showed them around the store, but I had a business proposition for the Hall of Famer. "Rod, I read that you didn't do any card shows, but now I see you're doing one at Regina High School in Minneapolis. I would have asked you to come here if I would have known. I would like to offer you the same amount of money that you receive for this appearance and have you come here next year."

"I'll tell you what I'll do," he said. "And this is the only way I'll do a card show for you. I'll come here next year and do a signing for you, but I don't want any of the money. You just pay my airfare. Anytime, you would like me to do the show, just let me know."

This, of course, was an incredible offer. Rod was

getting twenty dollars per signature at the Regina card show.

I didn't think he was completely serious. "You've got to be crazy. I'll pay you."

Rod took a sip of his Pepsi. "You were so nice to me throughout the years. This is one way I can pay you back. And this is the only way I'll do a show for you."

The day he made this offer, he insisted on signing a couple dozen baseballs for us to sell in the store. He was very aware of how valuable his scribbling was to fans, and wanted to give me a gift. In addition, he signed dozens of autographs free and posed for pictures with the customers who were in the museum or store at the time and discovered his identity. The day before he had been getting twenty dollars a clip and had people standing in lines.

In the off season, before his appearance in my store, Rod became a batting instructor for the California Angels. I was concerned that the deal was null and void with his new occupation, because the Angels tried to prohibit Rod from doing card shows. He was being offered $20,000 for a show on the East coast and the Angels said he couldn't go to it. Rod told them, "Fine, you pay me the extra money, and I'll stay here." The team decided they could spare him.

I decided it would be best for me to call him and check

on our deal. Rod said, "It's the same deal as I said, keep the autograph fees, and I'll sign for two hours."

In the next few months, my youngest son, Ray, was in constant touch with Carew concerning the show. Mainly they went over the times and items that Rod did not want to sign. He wouldn't sign bats or jerseys, or Legend items. Legend is a publication that features retired ball players. Yet, the publication neglects to give any proceeds to the athletes. As a result, many players won't sign their items. The lack of an autograph on one of these items severely cripples their value.

He arrived at the store/museum on September 12, 1992 and signed for two hours without charging me anything. He talked and joked with people the entire time he was there, and they seemed to really enjoy meeting him.

Someone mailed in a small baseball to have Rod sign. It was the size of a ping-pong ball. Rod said, "This is what the ball looks like when you're in a slump." Everyone in line enjoyed his insight. He is without a doubt one of the most super people ever to be involved with baseball. He was moody at times but sincerely amongst the nicest and best ball players in the history of organized baseball. He truly deserves to be in the Hall of Fame.

* * *

Dave Boswell, my former roommate, and I met in an unusual way. The first time I saw him was in spring training when he came from Baltimore. Jim Wiesner and I were at Tinker Field near the batting cage down the right-field line. We saw someone running alone in the field. The man was wearing a suit and street shoes, and looked like he was doing laps.

I pointed at the man. "Jim, get that guy off the field."

It wasn't that unusual to have fans run around the field acting like they were in the big leagues. Often there were bets or offers of beer involved in the dare.

Wiesner went after the guy and returned. "That guy says he's a ball player that was invited to spring training. He says his name is Boswell."

"All right, don't worry about it." I remembered seeing a Dave Boswell on the spring training roster. He didn't make the team that spring, but we became very good friends and roommates. In fact, he was in my wedding party in 1965 and I was best man in his wedding.

I was married on the morning of September 25, 1965, went to our Twins/Senators game in the afternoon, and had a sit-down reception that night. We were one game away from winning the American League pennant. Dave Boswell and Jim Lemon were the only members of the team permitted to come to the reception, but the entire team had been invited. The rest of the team awaited the outcome of the Baltimore game. If the Orioles lost, the Twins would have won the pennant.

My father had tuned into Baltimore's game during the reception and discovered that Baltimore was about to lose. I asked my new bride if it would look bad if I went to the team's victory celebration. She looked dumbfounded, but quickly added, "I guess you'll have to take care of that party and I'll take care of this one." I knew she would be disappointed by my departure, but it was a very exciting time for the ballclub. Fortunately, Baltimore came back and won the game. The reception continued as planned, and the Twins won the pennant the next day.

After the wedding, Carol flew to Minnesota with us and was to share the apartment with me. Then, Dave Boswell was still my roommate and frantically tried to find a place to stay, but nothing was available. He was stuck with the newlyweds. Carol was okay with the situation. Dave wasn't an outsider and he needn't have to look for a place to stay.

Carol was curious about one aspect of the apartment. She wanted to know why all the fuzzy fruit on the dinette was defaced by cryptic scribblings. She thought that Dave's autograph on the fruit amounted to a large ego, or a ritualistic act of ascribing possession. The truth of the matter is that I felt Dave's signature was so poor he'd ruin the baseball so I made him practice on the fuzzy fruit.

When Boswell entered the big leagues, his high school record was 44-2. He had signed for a $15,000 bonus with the Twins, which was very large in those days. The Twins had planned on making Boswell a starting pitcher. He asked the manager, Sam Mele, if he could start in his hometown of Baltimore. To go even further, he wanted to start against Wally Bunker since Boswell lost by a nose to Wally in the draft. The pitcher even used gate receipts as an incentive to get Mele to let him start. It is, after all, a business. Boswell said, "Sam, if you let me start against Wally Bunker, we'll pack the entire ball park."

Sam was interested in Boswell's marketing philosophy. He had heard a lot in his time and wanted to know why Boswell thought the stadium would be packed.

"If Wally pitches," Boswell explained. "All his friends will come watch. And if I pitch, all my enemies will come watch me get my butt kicked. Between the two groups, the place will be loaded with people." Mele just shook his head and walked away. Boswell couldn't convince Sam to let him start on this occasion.

Dave finally started when the team went to Boston. The first batter lined a single to right on the first pitch. The second hitter hit a rope to left, also on the first pitch. The next batter crushed his first offering against the centerfield wall for a double. Three pitches, three rockets that amounted in two runs with zero outs. Sam came out to the mound with the catcher, Earl Battey. Sam said, "Earl, what do you think?"

Battey looked at Sam and then at Dave. "I don't know, I haven't caught one yet." It was an honest reply.

After that comment, Boswell looked toward the batter and turned to Battey. "Is this guy a first ball hitter?" Earl smiled and laughed, but that was typical of Dave Boswell.

When we left Boston for Cleveland, Boswell pitched again during the series. He walked the first three batters and obviously was struggling in his second career start. Mele came out to the mound and Boswell said, "Don't worry Sam, I can get this guy out."

Sam pointed to first base, second base, and then third base. "Why didn't you get these guys out?"

Boswell followed Sam's finger. "Don't worry, it's only Rocky Colavito." Rocky was a great hitter, but Boswell was right. He stuck out Rocky and the next two batters. Sam Mele smiled, and didn't know what to say.

* * *

Boswell and I lived directly beneath an apartment rented by the Control Data Corporation. Boswell liked to go to sleep very early when he was pitching the next day. Calvin never believed it, but Dave would go to sleep at eight o'clock before day games. He may have stayed up until two in the morning after he pitched, but always went to sleep early when he was pitching.

The owner of the building, whom we rarely saw, knocked on our door at seven in the morning.

"Is Dave here?"

I was just barely awake. "Yes, but he's still sleeping. He's pitching today."

The man insisted that I awaken him since he wanted to talk to him about the previous night. I looked around the apartment trying to find something out of place. I looked all over the floor, but didn't find a thing in disarray.

Apparently, the people who lived in the apartment above us had a loud party the night before and Dave went up to ask them to keep the noise down. When he went back to our apartment, the people turned up the stereo even louder and began stomping on the floor. Dave was famous for his affection for firearms, and went back upstairs to confront the noisemakers with pistol in hand.

When the people answered the door he waved the gun in the air like Wyatt Earp. He said, "Look, I asked you nicely to keep the noise down. I'm trying to sleep. Let me tell you one thing. I'm going to go back downstairs. Every time I hear someone stomping on the floor, I'm going to put a hole through the ceiling."

Dave went back downstairs and got a good nights sleep. The next day, all six guys that lived in the apartment moved out and told the owner their reason. One of them had said, "I was afraid of falling out of bed and getting shot to death."

When I was in charge of the visiting clubhouse, I met Ted Williams. There have been many myths about Williams being a great tipper. The media made a big story about the World Series in 1946 when Ted Williams gave his World Series check to the clubhouse man. They neglected to tell the important aspect of the story.

The clubhouse manager was Johnny Orlando, and the check was for approximately nine hundred and fifty dollars. Williams made a big deal out of giving his check to Orlando in front of the press. The press took off on this act and assumed that he tipped the clubhouse man his entire World Series share.

The press didn't report that Williams never paid his bills until the end of the season. In that particular season, he owed Orlando eight hundred dollars or more. Thus, the tip wasn't as big as the press made it out to be.

I had similar experiences with Williams and his thriftiness as the visiting clubhouse manager in Washington. Whenever the Boston Red Sox came to Clark Griffith Stadium, we always had a full house. Sammy White, who was Boston's catcher and player representative, told the players that the proper tip was ten dollars per day plus expenses. Ted Williams used to come into the clubhouse on the first day and write out a check to "Ray Crump" for thirty-five dollars. He would hand me the check and I remember he never wrote it in his checkbook. I assume he had so much money that he didn't have to worry about bouncing a check, or perhaps he was a Congressman. Anyhow, after handing me the check, he would then ask for twenty-five dollars back.

I spoke with other clubhouse managers, and they all said he did the same thing with them. The thing that really irritated me was that he used the returned check to use for a tax deduction. Thus, he declared that he gave us more than he actually did and wrote it off on his taxes. So, while all the other players tipped me thirty dollars each for the weekend, Williams

72

only tipped ten.

It may sound petty to be concerned about a small tip, but clubhouse men depend on tips for much of their salary. It also didn't make sense that the richest man in baseball tipped the least. Often when players made the big salaries, they would tell the clubhouse man that their agent would take care of the tip. Williams and his meager tips really bothered me. I talked to the other clubhouse men, who all felt helpless. "What can you do, it's Ted Williams?"

I was undaunted by their words. "Well, I'll tell you one thing. He's not going to do it to me again."

On the next trip the Red Sox made to Washington, Ted Williams came up to me with his check book. I said, "Look Ted, if you want twenty-five dollars in cash make out the check to 'cash.' And if your writing the check out to me, then write 'Ray Crump.'"

Williams was very upset and his teammates looked toward the newly formed scene. The players supported me in this uprising, since they knew Williams ripped off clubhouse men around the league. Instead of arguing with me, Williams declared, "I don't have to give you nothing." With those words, he stormed off.

I shouted after him, "Great, and I'm going to tell the

press that you're the cheapest guy in baseball."

Tom Dowd, the traveling secretary acted as a public relations director for Williams. He ran over and gave me money for Ted's expenses including a tip.

Russ Nixon owed me around seventy-eight dollars in clubhouse dues when he went back to Boston after playing for the Twins. I was probably the only clubhouse manager in baseball who was guaranteed by the owner to receive all the clubhouse dues, regardless of strikes or trades. I tried to handle clubhouse bill problems without going to Calvin every time. Normally, I would try to get a hold of the player instead of bothering Calvin. I tried on several occasions to get the money from Nixon, but I saw he didn't intend of fulfilling his obligation.

The next time Nixon came into town, I left a note on his locker. "Russ, this is the bill you owe me from last year: $78.80. I would appreciate it if you could pay me as soon as possible. Thanks, Ray."

I left the note on the first game of the homestand, but received nothing on the following games. I decided to take action on the final day of the homestand. I went to the visiting clubhouse during the game. I took every personal item in his locker and brought it to our clubhouse. I said to Jim Wiesner, who was running the visiting locker room, "When he pays me the money he owes me, I'll give him back his clothes." The game ended late and the players had only about twenty-five minutes to get from the stadium to the airport. This was before they took chartered planes for most of their trips.

The Red Sox players ran into the locker room and quickly showered. Russ saw his clothes were missing, and frantically searched for his belongings until Wiesner explained the situation to him. Tom Dowd, the traveling secretary, came running over to my locker in the home clubhouse. He said harshly, "Jim Wiesner tells me you took Russ Nixon's clothes. You have no right to do that, and I want them back immediately."

"As soon as I get the $78.80 he owes me, I'll give back his clothes. If he doesn't he can go back to Boston nude!"

Tom face turned a bright red. "You can't take someone's clothes. I'm going to tell Calvin Griffith!"

I tried to cooperate in his request. "I'll give you his telephone number. He lives in Wayzata and it takes him about forty-five minutes to get home. So you'll have to give him some time to get there."

Dowd was fuming now. "Hey, how much does he owe

you?"

"Seventy-eight dollars and eighty cents."

He took the money out of his pocket and paid me.

"Great, now if you do an about face, you will see his clothes in the locker behind you."

Brant Alyea played for the Minnesota Twins in the early seventies. I had heard that he had a habit of passing out bad checks. We got to the end of a season and he owed over four hundred dollars in clubhouse dues, for which he handed me a check. I called the bank, which happened to be the same bank to which I belonged. Normally, they wouldn't have checked, but I knew an executive there who looked up Alyea's account for me.

"Ray," he said solemnly. "He doesn't have the money in his account, but you can't tell him that I told you."

"Okay, thanks. Don't worry about it, I won't say a thing." And I hung up the phone.

The next day, I sat next to Alyea's locker and spoke very quietly, "Brant, you know, it's so close to the end of the season. I would rather have cash than a check."

He jumped up and exclaimed, "What's the matter, don't you trust me? Do you think I'm going to give you a bad check? I'm not going to run out on you!"

A few players turned toward us.

"Brant," I said calmly. "I know your not going to run out on me. I have only had one ball player run out on me and that was Walter Bond. And he ran out on me because he died. So as long as you don't die, your not running out on me."

Walter Bond had died early in his life due to leukemia. The club released him right before his death and he was very upset. He complained to Tom Mee. "They said that I'm sick! I'm not sick!" Three or four months later, he went to the big baseball diamond in the sky.

Brant paid his bill with cash and didn't say another word.

Dean Chance was the best tipping ballplayer I had with the Twins. He was traded to us on December 2, 1966 with Jackie Hernandez for Jimmie Hall, Don Mincher, and Pete Cimino. I called the Angels equipment manager, as I always did when we received new players, to get uniform sizes. He told me the size and added that I shouldn't worry about Dean Chance. In other words, I shouldn't go out of my way for him. He said, "He's a lousy tipper, and I wouldn't waste your time on him."

Often, an equipment manager would spend extra time on

a player doing various errands. Then, he would leave without a decent tip. Tips, were a vital part of the salary of clubhouse workers. I was somewhat concerned with this revelation so I asked Jim Wiesner, since he dealt with him in the visiting clubhouse. Jim said, "He's cheap. He won't give you nothing."

When the season started, Dean came to me and said, "I pay my bill at the end of the season, so don't worry. When the season is finished you'll get paid." This wasn't that unusual. Many players chose to pay after the season, rather than be bothered several times throughout the season. During the year, I found Chance to be amongst the most trouble-free ballplayers I ever had. He was the type of player that when you told him you couldn't locate his uniform, he said, "I don't care just give me any uniform. Don't worry about it." Other ball players would throw a tantrum if things didn't go their way. Dean was such an easy going ball player that after the season I really didn't care how much I was tipped by him.

Near the end of the season Dean asked, "Can you tell me how much money I owe you?"

I looked up his record and answered, "Yes, you owe me $611.30."

Dean took out his wallet and placed money in my hand

like "Let's Make a Deal." He said, "Here's one hundred, two hundred, three hundred, four hundred, five hundred, six hundred, eleven dollars, and thirty cents."

I began to walk away, when he called me.

"Wait a minute. That's just your bill." He filled my hand again. "One hundred, two hundred, three hundred, four hundred, five hundred, six hundred, seven hundred, eight hundred, nine hundred, one thousand dollars." It was a very generous tip, normally I was only given a couple hundred for a tip at the end of the season. It's ironic that the more a player made, the less he tended to tip.

I was sitting in a bar drinking a screwdriver, to show another generous side of Dean Chance. Each drink was only a dollar, a far cry from today. I had a couple of drinks when the waitress came over and brought me two more.

"What's this?" I asked.

She placed the drinks on the table. "I don't know, but some guy just passed by and gave me twenty-five dollars and a ten dollar tip and said keep your drinks coming." I found out later that the benefactor was Dean Chance.

Dean was on the disabled list when the team went on a road trip. I wasn't making that trip and he asked me if I wanted to make three hundred dollars.

"If you run with me every day the team is on the road, I'll give you three hundred. I would have blown three hundred on this trip anyhow, so I might as well give it to you."

I agreed, and met him at the stadium at nine as we were going to do every day. We ran from the foul line to the outfield and then walked back. This exercise was typical of the pitcher's workout. We repeated this exercise thirty-five times. We were supposed to meet every morning at nine.

The funny thing about the workout is that everyone came out to watch. I hadn't been known for working out with the team. Calvin, Howard Fox, and other office employees sneaked out of the office and watched this rare track event. The next day, I woke up and couldn't get out of bed. My limbs felt like cement and I thought the bed was filled with quick sand. I finally dragged myself into the stadium looking like the Hunchback of Notre Dame.

I told Chance to start without me and I would eventually join him. I decided it would be best to take a whirlpool bath, and then go out to the field for continued torture. I had been involved with major league baseball for many years, but had never gotten into the whirlpool. After being in the tub until my skin pruned, my aches and pains dissipated. The soothing jets made my body feel good as new and I decided that I was healthy enough to run with Dean.

When I got to the field my joints stiffened up again. I was unable to move with any finesse. I felt like the tin man running out of oil. Dean handed me three hundred dollars and said, "Thanks, you tried." He wasn't really disappointed that I couldn't run with him. Rather, he saw that I honestly gave it my best effort. Fans often take for granted how much work players must do to be in shape. From experience, I know it's not easy. It was a good thing that everyone saw me run the first day, since it was my last.

Pete Sheehy was the equipment manager for the Yankees for sixty years. In 1962, the year after Roger Maris hit his record 61st home run, Sheehy felt very ill. He was so sick that he neglected to pack Maris' uniform during spring training. Since Maris had accomplished his amazing feat the previous year, Roger was hounded by the press. I was concerned that Sheehy would get in trouble for forgetting the uniform and decided to help. I asked Maris if he would mind wearing a windbreaker until we made a new uniform for him. Maris agreed and the press was never the wiser. Pete Sheehy was so grateful he acted like I was a king.

I saw Pete Sheehy again while I was in New York on a

road trip, and I needed to take the Eastern shuttle to Washington. I planned to take a cab to the airport when Pete told me that one of the players would give me a ride. Al Downing lived close to the airport and agreed to give me a ride. He dropped me off at the airport and they said I was in the wrong terminal to catch the Eastern flight. I had about fifteen minutes to make the flight and the woman at the counter suggested that I take a taxi to the other side of the airport. I ran outside and jumped into a cab.

"Where to?" Said the driver carrying a large smile.

"The Eastern shuttle."

His smile disappeared. "You son-of-a-bitch. I waited in that line for two hours to take you two city blocks."

"You just blew your tip." I stated simply, but I arrived in time for my plane.

While I was with the Twins, my pay consisted of: a salary, clubhouse dues, and tips. Generally, the clubhouse dues early in my career consisted of seven dollars a week. The players would pay me this fee for taking care of their personal items, doing laundry, etc. One year I was audited by the Internal Revenue Service, because some players reported that they gave me a lot more money than they actually did.

I went to the Federal Office Building in Minneapolis to

meet with the IRS. The first day I went there I pulled up to the parking lot and the attendant asked, "Sir, will you be long?"

"No, not too long." I was hoping.

When you were not going to be in the building long, the attendant would give you a parking spot up close. I arrived with armfuls of clubhouse record books, but the agents requested more notes and receipts. The next day I went back with additional records, and the parking lot worker asked me the same question. "Sir, will you be long?"

"No, not too long." I responded apprehensively, because I was getting to be unsure.

For the second time, the agents requested more documents. On the third day I returned with a large box containing every receipt and document I could find. The parking lot attendant again asked me the now familiar question, "Sir, will you be long?"

"About three years." I answered sarcastically as I was a little too familiar with this attendant.

Finally, the IRS agents were satisfied and they granted me a $133 refund. They said, "We shouldn't have you in here. We should have these ball players audited." Later, they did audit certain players.

Jim Kaat approached me once, because he had a problem

with the IRS. He said, "My accountant says we need a receipt stating that you received a six hundred dollar tip last year."

I said, "I'll check my records and give you a receipt." I knew he hadn't given me that much of a tip.

He handed me a self-addressed stamped envelope to send the receipt to his accountant. I looked in the clubhouse books for the full season and found that Kaat had tipped me only $5.85. I took a piece of Minnesota Twins stationary and wrote: "I received, as a tip from Jim Kaat, the amount of $5.85. This was for shining his shoes (480 pair), doing his laundry (200 days), taking care of his mail, and doing various errands throughout the season." I placed the letter in the envelope and sent it to the accountant.

After practice, Kaat approached me and asked, "Did you take care of that?"

"Yes, I wrote the receipt and sent it out to your accountant." I didn't bother to mention to him the amount I had written.

Kaat's accountant got back to him and said, "We can't send this to the IRS. Ray did all this work for you and you only tipped him $5.85." At least after that occurrence, Kaat began to tip better. He increased his gratuity from under ten dollars to around $160 a season.

The players would occasionally get into this kind of trouble. They would document a taxi ride when they really took the bus, and other indiscretions. It often turned out that the IRS would come after the little guys, the equipment managers, instead of the players who made the large salaries.

I was in charge of choosing which players would have lockers next to one another. Normally, if players were friends, I would place them next to each other. For example, Mudcat Grant and Earl Battey were friends and their lockers were together. Their lockers were placed together because of friendship, not race. After ball games, the reporters would flock around the pitcher's and catchers to get their views on the game. Mudcat Grant approached me and asked if he and Earl Battey could exchange lockers with the bat boys, who were in a back corner in the locker room. He wanted to escape from the reporters after a bad game. I agreed and the players and bat boys switched lockers.

The Twins traded Mudcat to the Los Angeles Dodgers in 1967. *Sports Illustrated* had an article about the trade, in which Mudcat made some disparaging remarks about the organization. He mentioned having his locker moved to the back of the locker room. He requested the move, but he made it appear that their were racial undertones in his locker placement.

My mother told me that the magazine had called me at her home in Virginia, and they wanted me to return their call collect. I didn't get around to calling them back, until I went to spring training. Bob Willis, the Twins general manager in Orlando, said *Sports Illustrated* had called. They were calling to confirm the rumor that racial motivations led to Mudcat's locker location. I told the reporter, "That's a damn lie. I put him back there because that was the way he tipped." There wasn't any mention of racism in the April, 1968 article.

Mudcat was shagging balls in the outfield when the Dodgers came to Orlando for a game. He saw me in the dugout and ran over. "Ray, I swear I didn't say what the reporter said." I believed him. He is a first class guy. We were in the military together in Fort Knox, Kentucky, and he's done a couple of card shows for me in Minnesota.

Rich Reese was the honoree of a bachelor's party being held at a bar called "The Bullpen" in Hopkins. I was changing in the locker room to go to the party, when I received a message that someone was in the bullpen behind centerfield. I went to investigate the intruder and discovered Cesar Tovar was sitting by himself behind the centerfield wall next to the area the pitchers used to warm up.

"Cesar, what are you doing?"

He was happy to finally see someone. "Where's the party? I've been waiting. Where is everyone? They tell me it's in the bullpen."

I laughed, but he looked confused. "No, it's not here. It's in the bar called, 'The Bullpen.' You can follow me over there." He was relieved at my revelation since he had been there for over an hour.

When the Minnesota Vikings football games were held at Metropolitan Stadium during the Twins season, we had to empty the lockers. We would pack up each locker and put the items in big boxes, which were labeled with the player's name. Craig Kusick, the Twins first baseman in the seventies, was looking for his shoes and was really upset that he couldn't find them. Often, players were very particular about their personal items. They have game gloves, shoes, and other superstitious items. We checked the box, but found nothing. Craig and I looked through his locker, for a sign of his missing shoes. He stopped, looked at me and said, "Promise you won't tell anyone this."

"Sure, what?"

He smiled, pointed down to his shoes, and said, "I'm

wearing them." An interesting addition to the story--Craig Kusick is now a school teacher in Rosemount, Minnesota.

Ron Kline pitched for the Twins in 1967. Every two weeks he received quite a large check from the ball club, and I would get it cashed. He asked me to hold his money for him, because he was afraid of spending everything. I reluctantly agreed and handled all his finances during the season. He would ask me to send checks to his wife from time to time, or give him spending money. I started to get nervous, since I hid the money in the locker room and it was approaching twenty thousand dollars.

We were sitting in the clubhouse talking and I said, "You know I think we are going to be in the playoffs this year."

He looked at me with disbelief. "Man, what have you been smoking?"

We were multiple games back in the standings, but I thought we looked good. Rich Reese walked in the room wearing alligator boots. Kline asked, "How much did you pay for those boots?"

"Three hundred dollars."

Kline turned to me and said, "If we make it to the playoffs, I'll buy you a pair of alligator boots."

During the off season, Kline was released. I was sad to see him leave, but at least I didn't have to worry about watching his money. Often, when a player is released or traded, they didn't tip since they weren't going to see the equipment manager the next season as was the case with Russ Nixon. In Kline's case, he paid me all the clubhouse dues before he left, and in December he sent a Christmas card. In the card was a check for three hundred dollars and a note instructing me to buy the boots. The Twins tied for second place that year, but still received bonus money for finishing in the top three positions.

At the end of a season, Luis Tiant approached me and said with his thick Spanish accent, "Raymond, I want to leave this bicycle here with you. And if I no come back here next year, you keep bicycle. You give to your kids."

I agreed to take the bike and I put it on top of the sauna in the clubhouse at Met Stadium. I didn't think that it was any big deal since players often left stuff around until the next season. In this case, it was a little strange, since Tiant made such a big deal out of it.

Later, I was talking to Calvin. I don't know how we got on the subject, but Luis Tiant became the topic. I told Calvin, "Luis Tiant left a bicycle here. He said if he didn't come back with the club, I should give the bike to my kids."

Calvin responded, "You give that bike to your kids. There is no way that Tiant is coming back here next year. You might as well give it to your kids now, so they can enjoy it."

In November, 1970, I took Calvin's advice and took the bicycle home. When December and the baseball meetings rolled around, Tiant was still with the team. By this time, my kids and their friends had used the bike and it was beginning to show signs of wear and tear. I was starting to get a little worried, because I thought Tiant might come back with the team.

I expressed my concerns with Calvin who said, "Don't worry about a thing. He'll be gone by spring training. In fact, you can give his number to some other player."

Giving a number away was usually a death wish for a player, so I felt a little more secure. But, we entered January and he was still with the club. I packed and left for Orlando, and he still hadn't been traded or released. I started to pay a little more attention to the ads in the Sunday paper for bicycles.

Soon, it was February and the lockers were all prepared for the incoming players in March. When the pitchers and catchers arrived, Luis Tiant was among them. I was very concerned now. I was hoping for a bad outing when the Grapefruit League games began.

Three days before we broke camp and went back to Minnesota, I talked to Calvin up in his office at Tinker Field. As I was in his office, Calvin called Joe Cronin, the president of the American League. Calvin's sister, Mildred, had married Cronin. Calvin said to his brother-in-law, "I'm going to release two players. I'm releasing Dave Boswell and Luis Tiant."

Tiant's arm was so bad, that it was painful for him to comb his hair. Cronin told Calvin, "You can't release them now. It's too late. You break camp in three days. You should have released him three days ago."

"I have to release him," Calvin said as he looked at me packing his files. "If I don't release him, it's going to cost me a bicycle. And, I'm not buying a new bicycle."

Calvin laughed and Cronin asked, "What do you mean?"

"It's a long story," Calvin smiled. "But, if I keep Luis Tiant, it's going to cost me a bike."

Tiant and Boswell were released. Boswell caught on with Detroit. After playing triple-A ball in Richmond, Tiant rejuvenated his career in Boston.

Later in his life, Al Worthington was against people drinking and smoking.

This was a change and even a contradiction from his

early years when he used to drink like a fish. He told me that the day he stopped drinking was when he was with the San Francisco Giants. He had to speak at an engagement and was nervous so he had a few drinks to calm himself. He didn't feel any different, but when he started to give his speech, he sobered up completely. Ever since then, he hadn't taken another drink.

When we would take trips during spring training, we would bring a cooler full of beer with us for the drive back. When a player took a beer, we would write his name down as part of his clubhouse dues. I would shout to Al in the back of the bus, "Hey Al! Do you want a beer?"

He shouted a reply. "Take that beer and put it under the front tire of the bus and take off."

Another time on a trip to Vero Beach and the Dodgers, I took Worthington's uniform out of his bag. In its place I put a six pack of beer. When we arrived at the stadium, he looked for his uniform and yelled for me. He was really upset. "Ray, Ray, Where's my uniform? I know I packed it."

I let him worry about it for a few minutes before I returned his uniform to him.

I used to tease him often about his aversion to alcohol. A friend of mine, Ernie Pesis, also made the road trip with the team to California. While we were on the plane, Al came up and asked, "What are y'all going to do on your day off?"

"We are going to Las Vegas."

Al thought this was terrible. He shook his head like a Sunday preacher. "Horrible. Awful. That's disgusting. Why would anyone go to that shameless town?"

"Nah, you're crazy, it's not a sinful city. You just think it is."

A stewardess walked down the aisle serving drinks. I said, "Let me ask you a question. What do you think of Las Vegas?"

"I love it."

I continued, "What do you think of drinking?"

Again she answered, "I love it."

Al looked at the woman and said, "Sinful. Sinful. People like you are going to hell."

She smiled. "Well, if I go to hell, I'm going to die drinking in Las Vegas with a smile on my face."

Worthington wouldn't believe that we hadn't put her up to it. He probably still thinks it was a set-up. He preached to me for a few years, but finally gave up. I guess he thought I was going straight into the hellfires anyhow, so he was wasting his breath.

* * *

I have gone to the induction ceremonies in Cooperstown, New York on three separate occasions. Each year they held the ceremony on a Sunday, and then Monday they would have "The Hall of Fame Game." This game featured an American and a National League team and was held every year since 1940. The only year there wasn't a game was 1945, due to wartime restrictions. We flew into Utica, New York, and stayed overnight at a motel. When I was there, there was not much to do along the lines of entertainment. The whole town consisted of the motel and the airport. The most exciting thing to do, when I was there, was to go to the airport and watch the blinking lights of the pinball machine. However, I wasn't there for the night life. I was going to the ceremony.

We went to Cooperstown in 1982 for a game against the Phillies in August. Mr. Griffith gave me a ball to be signed by Hank Aaron, who was attending the game. Aaron was eventually inducted into the Hall of Fame. Calvin wanted the ball signed to Philip, who was his son-in-law and the owner of the Pillsbury corporation. I walked onto the field to get the autograph and waited for the people who were standing around Aaron to finish their business. When they did, I walked up, handed him the ball, and said "Mr. Aaron would you please sign this to Philip?"

I was wearing my Twins uniform, so he could tell I was with the ball club, rather than simply a fan. He didn't seem interested in giving me his signature. In fact, he grimaced at my simple request.

"Man," he said. "I don't sign to anybody. I just write my name."

I said. "Jam that baseball up your ass!" After making my feelings apparent, I walked away without another word.

Mr. Griffith was up in the stands during the incident. He asked me if I got the ball. I told him that I didn't get his signature because he wouldn't sign it to "Philip."

He said, "That's okay, it doesn't need to have Philip on it."

"No it's not. I told him to take the ball and jam it up his ass."

We went home after the game, and arrived in Minnesota at ten or eleven o'clock. I went immediately to the ballpark to unpack the bags.

I finally got home at two or three in the morning, and I wasn't in a good mood. We had tables and chairs at my house that Jim Johnston, who worked in the print shop at Metropolitan Stadium, made completely out of baseball bats. I asked Carol for a saw and when she brought it to me, I started sawing off a leg on a table that contained one of Hank Aaron's bats.

Ever since that happened, whenever we had people in our home they asked why the table only had three legs and we would have to tell them the whole story. One day, my wife became sick of all the questions and took another bat out of the garage. She attached the bat of Glenn Borgmann, who was a catcher for us in the 1970's, to the table so it would have four legs again. Borgmann was a good guy, but not a Hall of Fame ball player. Now, when people came to the house they would ask a new question. They asked why we had a Glenn Borgmann bat amidst the bats of Rogers Hornsby, Stan Musial, Mickey Mantle, and then Glenn Borgmann. So, I turned the table around so that Borgmann's name would be facing the wall. Currently, the tables are on display in my baseball museum in Minneapolis. Glenn Borgmann's name is still hidden from sight. Of course, my youngest son now criticizes me for making furniture out of the bats of Hall of Fame players. But, it doesn't bother me. I'm probably the only person in the world with a table made with the remains of these players' bats.

I never really cared for Dick Stigman, when he was a player for the Twins from 1962 to 1965. After Stigman left the Twins, he played a couple of more years in Boston. While at the

Minnesota State Fair, I came across a whirlpool bath company. There was a large sign stating that Stigman had a stake in the company. I said to the guy, "Let me ask you a question. If I get two of these, do I get a better deal?"

The man said "Sure you do. I'll give you a great deal."

Carol didn't know what I was doing and looked at me like I was crazy.

"Do you ship?" I asked.

"Sure we ship." The man started to spout a smile.

I asked Carol for the checkbook. She was still looking at me as though I was insane, but reluctantly handed me the checkbook.

I asked, "Whom do I make the check out to and for how much?"

He told me the name and amount, and I inscribed my check. I handed him the check and told him the desired destination of each whirlpool. Our business was complete and we walked away. A few steps later, I went back and asked to see my check. The salesman gave me the check and I asked, "Does Dick Stigman have anything to do with these pools."

The salesperson proudly stated, "Sure, he's part owner of the company."

I started ripping up the check and said, "Oh I didn't

know that." I threw the pieces in the garbage, and walked away again. The man had a completely blank stare on his face like he didn't know what had hit him, and I'm positive he went back to Stigman and told him what had transpired.

Racism was a very prevalent and pervasive force in the South during my early years with the Twins as it had been for years. On a long road trip during spring training, we used to stop at some point for lunch. Some of these restaurants refused to serve the black ballplayers, even after Jackie Robinson broke the race barrier and entered Major League Baseball from the Negro League. These players would have to sit on the bus while I brought their food out to them, which obviously was completely unjust. I would even suggest that we bring box lunches instead of eating in the prejudiced restaurants. We went to Kentucky Fried Chicken or other restaurants and saved time and money by eating on the unsegregated bus.

It was even worse when we had to stay overnight in a town. For instance, when we went to Miami, the hotels in the cities were segregated. The white players would stay in one hotel, while the black players would have to stay in the "black neighborhoods." The hotels in these neighborhoods were few and far apart, and often the players would have to stay in private residences. We would have to call ahead to try and accommodate the players who were unfairly excluded. I told Mr. Griffith that I thought it was unfair, and suggested that we could give the black players the station wagon to drive wherever they needed to go. This was a small concession, but it enabled the players to get around town with greater ease since cabs didn't like to go into these neighborhoods.

In Orlando, the team stayed at the Cherry Plaza Hotel, which barred blacks. There was a bell hop, who had worked at the hotel for years and came up with a proposal. He asked Calvin if he would move the team to a new hotel in the black neighborhood, which would be a place that all the players could stay. At the time the black players were living in houses all over town so Calvin agreed. Before that time, Calvin was very reluctant to move since most of the "black hotels" were second or third rate and Calvin wanted the team to stay at nice hotels.

The team moved to the new Sadler Hotel. It was small, but kept very clean and the players liked it. In fact, some players, like Earl Battey, were treated like kings or heroes in these areas. The team moved to a new multi-race hotel in Orlando called The Downtowner. Some black players didn't want to move, since they were treated so well in their current location and decided to keep a room in both hotels. It made sense to them since they ate in the area, their friends were there, and they felt more comfortable in that district. Sam Mele was asked about curfew, and who was watching the players. He said, "I don't care anything about their curfew. I'm not going to the area at one or two in the morning. If you're so damned concerned about their curfew, you go check on them."

Actually, the players didn't need monitoring. It was spring training during a time when a player could lose his spot for misbehaving.

There were some ways to get around the racism. I will always remember that my father and Earl Battey liked to go to the racetrack together. Battey would have to sit in the black section and couldn't go into the white section, nor could my father go into the black section. My father and Battey would get around these ridiculous rules by both going as close to the track as possible and at this point, there was only a small metal fence separating the two. Thus, they could watch the dog races together.

Battey and Don Mincher went to the Sanford Orlando Kennel Club. They pulled up to the valet stand and both went into the building. Battey pointed to the section of the track that was reserved for "Colored."

Mincher told Battey, "Well Earl, I'm going to go over to the other side."

Battey responded, "I can't go in there."

Mincher said, "Bullshit! You are with me. You can go in this section."

"No," he protested. "I can't go in there."

"Yes, you can." Mincher insisted and pulled him into the white section.

They walked down and stood by the fence where the dogs were thrust into their starting positions. A couple minutes later an usher approached them and he looked toward Battey. He said, "You can't be over here. Coloreds have to be on the other side of the fence."

Mincher replied angrily, "He's a friend of mine and he's staying right here."

"He can't stay here." The usher started to look a little nervous. "Look, I'm sorry, I don't make the rules."

"Well, who does?" Mincher asked.

"The manager, I'll go get him."

Very quickly, the usher returned with the manager. The manager reiterated to Battey, "You have to go on the other side of the fence."

Mincher refused to budge in his desire to keep Battey

near him. "You better get somebody bigger than that." He said, "You better get the head of the track."

By then, everybody near the scene was looking at the players and track personnel. The track owner, Jerry Collins, arrived and tried to break up the situation. Collins knew the men were professional ballplayers and directed them to follow him upstairs to his private box.

When they arrived, a huge buffet was offered. The track owner invited them to help themselves and then left. Mincher turned to Battey, smiled, and declared "Now, get your black ass back downstairs where you belong! I just wanted to get up here." They cracked up together.

Vic Power was given a ticket for jaywalking when he played for the Twins in 1963. Vic was on Orange Avenue and Church Street in Orlando when he walked across the street on a red light. The fine was five dollars, but he decided to fight the ticket in court. Earl Battey and several other ball players went into the court room, because they were sure to see a good show. Vic stood before the judge in his finest white Puerto Rican suit.

He said, "I don't speak English too good. But, I don't speak too bad neither. Now, I hear about all the segregation down here. I see white people cross when light is green. I figure we go when light is red. I don't want to get in no trouble."

The judge shook his head, "In my twenty-five years on the bench, I've never heard an excuse like that. I'm finding you not guilty, but I don't want to ever see you in court for jaywalking again." The players rolled in the benches laughing, and the case was dismissed.

Spring training always brought along interesting stories. One particular year, we had planned on meeting Herb and Kathy Carneal in Nashville, Tennessee. Herb was the Twins' broadcaster and we all liked country music. Unfortunately, the weather turned ugly and Marshall law was declared. We were told to either stop for the night or face a trip to jail. The Carneal's car was forced to stop for three days in a hotel, while I decided to venture further up the road.

Kathy had to take charge of the hotel since it's employees could not make it to work. She did a miraculous job in organizing food and rooms for three days. Meanwhile, I drove around several roadblocks and was finally forced to stay the night in a school which was turned into a shelter. Carol wasn't happy about my refusal to stop, but we made it to the Grand Ole Opry in record time.

* * *

When Mike Marshall joined the Twins' pitching staff in 1978, I called the equipment manager of the Los Angeles Dodgers. I wanted to find out his uniform size and how he tipped. He said, "44 shirt, 36 pant, and very cheap. He's a very bad guy for the clubhouse. Ask the guy from Texas." I took his advice and called Texas.

The Texas clubhouse man reiterated the words I had heard from Los Angeles. When Marshall arrived in Minnesota, I discovered that each of these men was absolutely correct. Marshall wanted to change things in the clubhouse almost as soon as he arrived in Minnesota. He wanted to remove the soft drinks in favor or fruit juices, and replace ice cream with yogurt. We would have been the only locker room in the country who didn't allow our players to have a Coke and a smile.

Marshall came up with this brilliant plan of how I should supply certain foods in the clubhouse, and also what I would be paid for this service. I thought this plan was too good to be true and I asked Fox if I was understanding it properly. He said, "You stand to come out so far ahead that you'd be foolish to pass up Marshall's deal!"

Marshall eventually became the player representative for the team. Meanwhile, I didn't think the players would react well to all the changes. I was sitting in the Twins Room during a December football game with my friends, Ernie Pesis and Chuck Roitenberg. Calvin was also in the room and called me over to his table. "What do you think about us signing Mike Marshall to a two-year deal?"

"I think that would be terrible, Mr. Griffith. It's worse than firing Billy Martin."

His face lit up with a combination of confusion and curiosity. "What do you mean by that?"

"If you sign Mike, you'll get rid of him before the end of his contract and you'll have to pay the rest of his contract. In the case of Billy Martin, you got rid of him without a contract and didn't owe him a cent."

"I would never sign him and not keep him. He'll be here," Calvin said sternly.

"Well." I still disagreed. "I think it's the worst thing you could do."

"I talked to Brad Corbett, the Rangers' owner. He said Marshall is a very good guy in the clubhouse."

I asked, "Mr. Griffith, is Brad Corbett a good friend of yours?"

"Yes, he's a very good friend of mine."

I spoke very sincerely. "Well, if he told you that

Marshall was good in the clubhouse, then he's a liar. I would never sign him."

This conversation took place Sunday. The next day, Howard Fox called me at home. In all the years I worked with the Twins, I only received a call from Howard at home on rare occasions. Fox was mad at me, because I told Calvin that I wouldn't sign Marshall. Fox knew that Calvin valued my advice and he had told Gene Mauch, the manager, that he wouldn't sign the pitcher. Mauch called Fox and complained to Fox, and he called because he was disgruntled with me for my conversation with Calvin.

Eventually, Calvin was pressured into signing Marshall. The next day, Calvin and Fox walked into the clubhouse while I was packing for spring training. They were holding a press conference to announce the signing of Mike Marshall's two year deal. Calvin said, "Do you want to come to the press room? They're serving food and announcing the new contract."

"No, I don't." They laughed and I reiterated my concerns. "Remember, Mr. Griffith, this is far worse then firing Billy Martin.

During the season, Marshall was pitching very poorly. He finished 1-3 for the season with 6.19 ERA. We were in the Twins dining room and Calvin said, "Raymond, your guy isn't doing too well."

I puzzled. "What guy is that?"

"Mike Marshall. He didn't pitch too good last night."

"Mr. Griffith, I told you a long time ago never to sign him. He's not 'my guy.'"

He looked me straight in the eye. "I better shut my god damned mouth up and just eat."

Actually, Clark Griffith, Bruce Haynes, Howard Fox, and Gene Mauch were the people in favor of the contract. The executives and manager pressured Calvin into making the deal. George Brophy, our farm director, agreed with me. Calvin pulled into the parking lot and got out of his car. He stepped out of the car and said, "Raymond, if I didn't listen to those son-of-a-bitchin' vice presidents, and only listened to you, I would be much better off." Later that day, he released the losing pitcher.

I used to have small black combs in the locker room, which the players would take in much the same way people pick up errant pens. To stem the pilfering of the combs, I purchased ugly multi-pack combs. They consisted of various sizes and colors like red, green and pink. My plan worked and there was always an abundant supply for the players. Wayne Granger, a pitcher and player representative for the team in 1972, kept a notebook of what he considered to be unfair practices. Amongst these atrocities were the lack of pens and small black combs in the clubhouse. He also wrote of "too many unnecessary night games" and "cold Minnesota weather." He was prepared to take this list with him to the players' union grievance committee.

Granger was on a road trip in Cleveland when he left his personal jacket on the field. He didn't bother to go back and retrieve it, which resulted in someone taking it. When he got back to Minnesota, he asked for a replacement. The baseball club supplied the uniforms, stirrups, socks, and team jackets. The player was required to buy his athletic supporter, t-shirts, jackets (without insignia), batting gloves and those types of items. The jacket that Granger lost was the type I sold, rather than the team jackets. When I replaced his coat, I billed him sixteen dollars.

When he received the bill in his mailbox, he shouted across the room, "You're a thief!"

I went after him and we had a little skirmish. The next day, we met in Calvin's office to discuss what had happened. I said, "I wasn't in Cleveland, and I should have been there. Because I wasn't there to pick up after him, he lost his jacket. Therefore, I'm responsible."

I didn't really feel as though I had to be there. Each

town had a visiting clubhouse man who was supposed to take care of the player's equipment. Yet, I wanted to get over the incident.

Calvin said to Granger, "The way you were acting, Ray should have taken a bat upside your head."

Granger said, "Yea, he should try that."

Things calmed down somewhat after the meeting. Calvin told me, "I would like to suspend that son-of-a-bitch, but we wouldn't get anything for him. But, I guarantee you, we'll get rid of him."

Granger remained with the team throughout the season. At the winter baseball meetings in Hawaii, Calvin approached me with glee on his face. "You owe me a bottle of wine. I got rid of that son-of-a-bitch, I traded him."

Tom Mee, the Public Relations Director, met me in the hallway a short time later. "Did you hear about a trade?"

"Yes, we got rid of Granger."

"Good," Mee said. "Calvin said he wanted to tell you about it first. He didn't want you to hear it second hand. Now I can issue the press release."

Occasionally, the players' wives provided amusing stories. Jim Kaat's wife, Julie, sat in the family section, behind home plate, at the Met. Although the seats were primarily for families and people associated with the club, regular fans could also buy tickets. Jim was struggling on the mound when someone shouted, "Get the bum out of there!" Julie didn't care for this proposal at all and began hitting the guy with her purse.

Julie was a very dedicated baseball wife. She recorded every pitch Jim made and let people know they made her miss a pitch if they happened to stand up and block her view.

Jim Roland's wife was preparing to drive to Minnesota with their two children. As Jim was saying goodbye, I said that maybe he should talk to Howard Fox first. Normally, Howard Fox didn't like me to tell players that they were being released. Yet, it didn't make sense for them to drive all the way to Bloomington when he wasn't making the trip up North.

Even though Jim was upset at what happened, his wife thanked me for saving her the trip. Jim caught on with Oakland in 1969 and continued to play in the major leagues for a few more years. It's kind of a trade off from keeping quiet like you are supposed to do and trying to help a family avoid a needless trip. I think that, in this case, I did the right thing. At least his wife appreciated my gesture.

The team was flying into Milwaukee, but the weather was too poor to land. Thus, they made a surprise landing in

Minnesota. When the players arrived at their homes, some of them discovered additional surprises.

When they arrived at home, they found babysitters with their kids instead of their wives. While people always talk about players having affairs while on the road, the wives often have secret romances also. It's a two-way street.

Mickey Mantle and I discussing baseball
before a game.

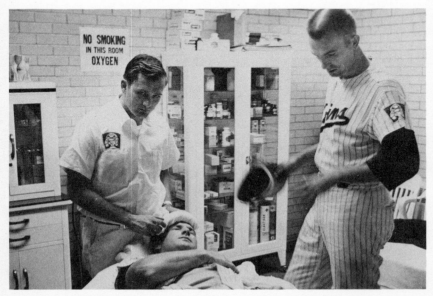

My job required me to act as a trainer at times. Here, I'm
attending to an injured Harmon Killebrew.

**Roger Maris, one of the best baseball players
of all time, and a great man.**

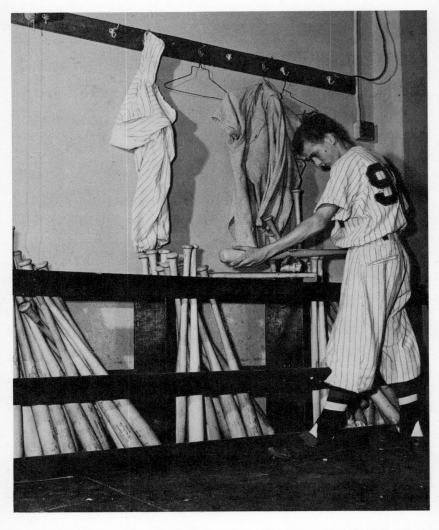

Ole Ninety-Seven "bones" a bat to make it smoother and stronger for harsh contact with a baseball.

You can learn a lot from a major leaguer like Mickey Vernon. I'm learning how to get a good grip on a piece of lumber.

**Ted Williams was one of the greatest players in the
history of the game, but a lousy tipper.**

Chapter 4

Coaches and Managers

When I was with the Senators, one of the managers was Chuck Dressen. We returned to Washington after a spring training barnstorming trip with the Chicago White Sox in 1956. We always started the season at home and the President of the United States would throw out the first pitch.

We had private cars on the trains, which would be pulled off the main track when we slept at night. Our catcher was Clint "Scrap Iron" Courtney, and he was known for always playing cards. Clint and some other players used to rent a hotel room to play cards after the ball games. When it got to be nine o'clock they would head off to the tracks to catch the train, which would leave a few minutes later.

My job was to do the roll call as the players got on the train. When I called off all the names, Clint was the only Washington player missing.

I yelled, "Has anyone seen Clint?"

Someone shouted and pointed in the direction of the hotel, "Yea, see that little light. He's in there playing cards."

I ran into the hotel to get him and said, "Come on Clint, you're going to miss the train." He nodded and I left. I assumed his nod was an acknowledgment of the impending departure of the train.

The train started to leave, and I jumped on the caboose.

Courtney couldn't be located on the locomotive. I walked up the train aisle, saw Dressen, and quickly hid in a drawing room. I didn't want to see the manager, because it would sound like I was snitching on Courtney. The train began to slow down and a man was out in front waving a lamp. When the train stopped, Courtney and the White Sox players from the recently completed card game jumped on board.

Dressen shouted, "Courtney! That's going to cost you two hundred-fifty." The fine was a very large amount for the players in the 1950s.

Clint replied in his Southern drawl. "Mister Dressen, I think you should check my contract. It says I have to take the team transportation, but it doesn't say a god damned thing about how far up the road I can catch it."

We found out later, the players had hopped into a cab and chased after the train. Actually, they commandeered the vehicle since it had been moving too slow. Courtney said "Let me drive and I'll take the tickets." He took over the wheel and they caught the train.

Courtney continued his argument with Dressen. "If you

fine me two-fifty, I'm going to have a piece of your ass."

Dressen dropped the matter, but they had a bitter relationship toward each other for the rest of the season.

In 1963, we had a bullpen coach named Joe Fitzgerald, who moved from Washington with us. I constantly played jokes on him, I especially remember once during a game against the Red Sox. Fitzgerald was down in our bullpen, in centerfield of Metropolitan Stadium, when I called him.

After he answered the phone, I said, "Get Radatz up." Fitzgerald didn't do anything since Dick Radatz played for the Boston Red Sox. Thus, he wasn't in charge of getting the opposing team's pitcher warmed up.

A few minutes later I called him back and shouted into the receiver. "What's the matter with you? I said I want Radatz to start throwing."

Joe thought something was wrong with the phone system. He walked to Boston's bullpen looking for their pitching coach. Fitzgerald shouted over the fence. "Johnny wants you to get Radatz throwing," referring to the Red Sox manager Johnny Pesky.

Radatz got up, took off his jacket, and starting warming up in the Red Sox bullpen. Pesky saw Radatz throwing and called down to their bullpen. He yelled into the phone, "Get Radatz down, sit him down!"

They relayed the message to Radatz and he stopped. About an inning after Radatz stopped throwing, I called Fitzgerald again. I yelled, "Get Radatz up! I want Radatz up!"

Fitzgerald tried without success to explain to me that I was getting the wrong bullpen. I ignored his explanations and continued to disguise my voice. He had no idea that I was calling him from the clubhouse. I shouted again, "Get Radatz up!"

Fitzgerald walked back over to the visitor's bullpen. He said to the Red Sox pitching coach, "I don't know what's going on, but they keep telling me to get Radatz throwing."

Radatz took his jacket off a second time and stepped on the mound. Johnny Pesky looked into center field and saw Radatz throwing again. He called again. "What the hell is going on down there! Get Radatz down!"

Boston's pitching coach was really bothered. He called Fitzgerald over the fence and shouted, "Listen, you take care of your players and we'll take care of ours."

Fitzgerald didn't know what had hit him and until I wrote this book, I never told anyone that I was the one calling the bullpen.

* * *

Another pitching coach for us, Don McMahon, used to stay in a motel on Portland and Interstate 494 in Bloomington and walked to the stadium. When he would get to Cedar Avenue, he had to jump a large fence that was supposed to prevent people from running across the road.

I decided to play a prank on him with the help of a friend who was on the Bloomington police force. I had my friend drive up to him in a cruiser after he jumped the fence.

They got into a big fight about the legality of hopping the chain links and the laws regarding trespassing. Finally, after a stern warning, the officer allowed our pitching coach to walk to the stadium. McMahon ran into the locker room and told me about being pulled over with flashing lights and blaring sirens. Even now, Don McMahon doesn't know he had been set up.

When Calvin Griffith fired Sam Mele in 1967, he had talked to Jim Kaat and a couple of other players in the morning and made the decision in the afternoon. Calvin wanted their advice about whether or not to dismiss the manager.

The owner didn't realize that the players had been manipulated by Johnny Sain, the pitching coach. The year before, Sam went to Calvin and asked him to fire Sain and Hal

121

Naragon. The pitchers loved Johnny Sain, since his contract said he never would have to take a player out of a ball game. Often a player had harsh feelings toward the person who was responsible for taking them out of the game, despite their performance. Yet, if someone was struggling on the mound, Sain would whisper to Mele, "Hey, he looks a little tired, I think you should take him out."

Sam would often follow Sain's advice, since Sain knew the pitcher's strengths and weaknesses, and remove the pitcher from the game. Johnny Sain followed the pitcher up the hallway into the locker room. He would tell the pitcher, "I don't know what Mele's problem is. He should have never taken you out of the game. I would have let you pitch, I don't understand him."

Of course, this caused animosity between the players and Sam. At the same time, the players liked Sain much more since the coach said he wouldn't have removed the player. Hal Naragon was nearly as bad. He was good friends with Sain and would rip Sam in front of the players. Both tried to be best friends with the players and alienate Sam.

Sam Mele found out about what as happening, and he wanted the coaches immediately fired. Calvin was very reluctant to fire them, since they were both successful and the players liked them. Many people have said that managers were jealous of Sain. More likely, they have been leery of what he did or said behind their backs. Loyalty is the most important thing in the managing of a baseball team. The Twins didn't have loyalty at the time, they had backstabbers. I always thought that if I were manager, I would want the best coaches around me, except in this case. Sain was very good, but deceptive. Chances are you'll be fired if you have a losing season, but you won't be fired if you win. If you have the best coaches working for you, the chances of winning are much better.

In the year Mele was fired, he called me at home early in the morning and asked me to come to the stadium. I got out of bed and drove to the stadium to meet him. I looked for Sam in the clubhouse, but he wasn't there. I walked down to the field, and saw him standing by himself with a fungo in the middle of the field. He looked very serious. "Ray, these people are playing terrible and I've got to do something. I want you to get rid of the sandwiches. I know this is going to cost you money, but I'm going to tell the players that they can have the sandwiches back when they play better."

This was right before Sam was dismissed and the team was struggling to play .500 ball. Sam was desperate enough to think that post-game snacks were damaging the team. He had been up worrying about how his plan to jump start the team would affect me. Sam's plan didn't change the way the team was playing. Mele was fired after posting a 25-25 record in 1967.

The next manager, Cal Ermer, was more successful. Toward the end of that season, the Twins had a chance to go to the World Series and they held a meeting in the press room. The meeting was to determine how to divide the post season money. More importantly, they decided if Sam would get a share. A huge fight erupted in the room with everyone shouting at each other. Everyone was arguing back and forth, Earl Battey, Dean Chance and others thought Sam should get a full share. Other players didn't think he should get anything, so they took a vote and Sam was voted out of his share.

On the plane ride to Boston, Billy Martin and Dean Chance told me that I should tell Sam what had happened since we were close. On the plane I was furious at the vote. We headed for Boston in a series that would decide the winner of the American League. I thought, "You know, I don't give a damn if the Twins win it or not. Those players are so damn cheap. I hope we lose it."

Then, it was unheard of to vote someone out of the money, especially someone who had done so much for the organization. After all, Sam had been a part of the team for the first fifty games. He took the team to the World Series in 1965 and had already participated in nearly a third of the season. In the end, it didn't matter. Boston kicked our butt, and they went on to lose in the World Series against St. Louis.

We still had to tell Sam about the vote. Mele, Dean Chance, Billy Martin and I all went out to dinner. While we were eating, Dean and Billy decided to go to the men's room and they signaled me to tell Sam the unfortunate news. I told Sam what had happened in Boston before the games. Sam felt very bad and to make matters worse, he had to face the reporters to tell them his feelings on being slighted.

I felt awful for Sam.

And I felt bad for Cal Ermer who was voted a share of the post season money by a very slim margin. He had been a very tough manager, but he softened because he wanted to make sure he received a part of the money. It was really sad, the players were just money hungry bastards. When the players in the sixties were earning a hundred thousand a year, the post season money didn't even mean that much to them. For managers, who earned significantly less, the money made a big difference.

When Cal Ermer was the Twins' manager, he used to

bring his two kids with him to the games. The kids were ten and twelve, and would come to every home game at four p.m.

Cal's wife would go into the Stadium Club and have a few drinks, and the kids would just hang around the locker room since they weren't allowed in the dugout during games. Eventually, the kids would get tired or bored and began to annoy the bat boys. They would push or spit on them and their work would suffer. I told the bat boys to pick up the kids and throw them into the lockers if they were bothered by them. I said not to do it in a mean way, just laugh like you're playing a game. Eventually, I hoped, the kids would get the message. The clubhouse was not a playroom. A little while later, I heard a loud thump from one of Ermer's kids being thrown in a locker.

The next day Ermer came in and said, "You know, the bat boys started pushing my kids around and threw them into a locker. You better tell those guys to start treating my kids better."

I looked him straight in the eye, "Cal, let me tell you something. Your kids come to the ball park at four o'clock. Then they'll stay here until midnight, and these are young kids. They started to push the bat boys around and spit on them. Let me tell you one thing, from now on leave your kids out of the clubhouse. I'll tell you something else, I don't get paid to be a baby sitter for your kids. You don't pay me for that. I'm the clubhouse man, not the baby sitter. So, leave your kids at home."

Ermer looked stunned and dismayed. I simply walked away without further comment. After I made the speech, Early Wynn, our eavesdropping pitching coach during that season walked over to me. "Ray, " he said. "I want to thank you and shake your hand. I'm really happy, you showed me some balls there. You should have told him that weeks ago."

Soon after this, we were at the checkout counter at the airport before a road trip. Mrs. Ermer came up to me and said, "Did Cal talk to you about the way those clubhouse boys were treating my sons?"

I responded, "Did Cal talk to you about what I told him?"

"No, he didn't."

"I told him," I said. "To keep your kids out of the locker room. I'm not a baby sitter. The kids can stay with you when they go to a game. They're not going to be in the clubhouse." With these words, the problem was solved.

Calvin Griffith was very upset when Dave Boswell had a fight in a bar in Detroit. He was even more upset when he discovered that he had fought Billy Martin. Calvin's temper was heightened since Martin shouldn't have been in the bar with Boswell. Calvin had a strict rule that the managers and players could not be in the bar at the same time. He said, "If you walk into a bar and the players are there, you walk out."

On this night, Boswell and Martin were both equally smashed. Bob Allison and a newspaper reporter were also in the bar. Martin and Boswell were arguing about Boswell not running his laps and they decided to take it outside. Once they were in the alley, the fight started. The newspaper reporter and Allison broke it up by holding back Boswell. When they restrained Boswell, Martin continued to punch him.

Calvin wanted to fire Martin on the spot, despite his success with the team. Firing Martin wasn't necessary, he would eventually fire himself.

Calvin used to take a nap every afternoon from 4:15 to 5:30, and he left specific instructions not to be disturbed. Whenever Calvin told Martin he wanted to see him, Billy would get upset because he didn't want anyone to meddle with his team. Billy must have had the same problem with George Steinbrenner. Martin knew about Calvin's naps, and used them to get back at the boss. He waited until he knew Calvin was sleeping and then banged on the door. Calvin opened the door with sleep in his eyes. Martin asked, "You wanted to see me?"

This irritated Calvin to extremes, along with Martin's constant insults about the front office staff. Martin was also a critic of Calvin's friends, George Brophy and Howard Fox. Calvin considered each of them very valuable employees. He didn't like these criticisms and especially Martin's knack for going to the press with them. An unwritten rule in baseball is never inviting the press into internal problems.

During the season, Martin was courting other teams, which also upset Calvin. Meanwhile, Sid Hartman wrote in his column that Martin was taking the team to the pennant and was untouchable despite his off-field indiscretions. Baseball club owners do not like outsiders telling them who they can and cannot get rid of. Hartman was right about one thing, Martin took them to the playoffs. It was 1969 and Baltimore swept the Twins in three games during the American League Championship Series.

Calvin arranged to meet with Martin after the season was over to discuss his future with the ballclub. Martin went hunting, and avoided Calvin like the plague. Calvin would call the clubhouse almost everyday and asked me if I had heard from Martin, or knew how to locate Martin. I didn't know how to get in touch with him, but finally Martin came into the clubhouse. I told Martin that Calvin was looking for him and he went up to Calvin's office and demanded a new contract and a raise. Calvin wouldn't give him any answer and he left town to watch the Orioles versus the Mets in the World Series. While Calvin was at the World Series, Hartman called him with a scoop delivered to him by Martin. "Billy says he doesn't have a job."

Martin was always trying to get publicity, and tried to stir things up by Calvin's refusal to give him an immediate answer. This was a way out for Calvin, who didn't know if he wanted him back.

Billy was a tough guy to handle, which is why he managed six different teams. He managed the Twins, Tigers, Athletics, Rangers, and of course, five different stints with the Yankees. I always said that if I owned the ball club and paid the manager a hundred thousand dollars a year, I would give Billy a hundred and twenty thousand to be an instructor. He knew the game, and could teach the game. He just couldn't handle the players or himself, which led to both his professional demise and ultimately took his life.

Martin loved the game, and he took all aspects of it very seriously. When the team lost, it was as though a vital organ had been extracted from his body. He went into the manager's office after a loss and violently kicked down the refrigerator. A glass on top of the appliance flew across the room and shattered. I rushed in to see what caused all the commotion. Upon seeing the refrigerator, I said, "Billy, that refrigerator is going to stay like that all season. Because I'm not picking it up."

During the night, I had a change of heart and was prepared to clean up the mess when I arrived at the stadium in the morning. Billy Martin was already there, several hours before he usually arrived, and he was cleaning up the pieces of broken glass. I always considered Billy a friend, I liked him despite his moods.

We used to have a few extra lockers in the clubhouse during the beginning of the season. It was my responsibility to bestow extra lockers to players who needed them. I would put a spare locker for personal belongings between Killebrew and Allison, since they came from Washington with the club. I gave another one to Tony Oliva. After the season, when we had the September call ups, I had to give away Oliva's second locker. I thought that Oliva was a great player, and perhaps the rookie could learn something from him. However, Oliva was very upset about losing his locker and complained to Billy.

Martin complained to me because of Tony's request to have an additional locker. There wasn't a chance that I was going to change the locker configuration due to Martin's request.

"Billy, I don't tell you how to run your ball club. I don't want you to tell me how to run my clubhouse."

Now the tough Billy Martin of the popular press would have punched me. He punched Boswell. He punched a marshmallow salesman. He punched friends. He punched a bunch of people. Billy respected me as a clubhouse guy and he knew I was right. He turned around walked back to the field and told Oliva that it wasn't going to happen. Even after Billy had left the club, he always returned to say "Hello" to me.

Billy used to always jump on the case of the players who didn't play everyday, and would leave the others alone. The only big name player, that I can remember, that he jumped on was Reggie Jackson. The only reason he picked on Jackson was for the publicity.

Billy loved publicity, which is why he got into so many fights with umpires. It was obvious to us, the people who worked behind the scenes, that Billy was just acting. After kicking dirt on an umpire in the game, Billy would go up to the locker room during the game and instruct us to put a bottle of booze in the umpire's bag. Either he felt sorry about his actions, or didn't want an umpire on his bad side.

Billy said to Doc Lentz and myself, "You know why fans come to the baseball games? They don't come to see the players, they come to see me." He honestly believed that. If he didn't get mentioned in *Sports Illustrated* or other publications several times a week, he wouldn't have been so demonstrative on the field. In the same way that John McEnroe revolutionized tennis, Billy changed baseball. Billy Martin will always be remembered as one of the true characters of the game.

Al Worthington approached me during the 1971 spring training with a message from the manager, Bill Rigney. Bill wanted Bert Blyleven and Jim Kaat to take the team station wagon to a game in Winter Haven, which was about thirty-three miles from Orlando. Blyleven and Kaat wanted to use the car so they could leave early and make it back in time for the Citrus Open Golf Tournament.

I said, "Al, that station wagon isn't going anywhere."

Al looked at me, "But, you're making the trip tomorrow, so no one will be using the car."

I agreed, "You're right Al. The car is going to be sitting at the ball park. You're one hundred percent right."

Al went back and Rigney, who became very irate at me and went to talk to Calvin. He told Calvin that I refused to let them use the station wagon. Calvin wanted to hear the whole story before making a decision. He turned and faced Rigney.

"Now what did you want to do?"

Rigney started to plead his case. "Well, the team is going to go over to Winter Haven on the bus. Blyleven and Kaat will use the station wagon to drive over there, so they can come back when the game starts. And Ray said that no one is going to use the station wagon."

Calvin said, "Yes, you're completely right. The station wagon isn't going to turn a wheel."

Rigney came back to me and I tried to explain my philosophy. "It's none of my business. I'm a clubhouse man. But, if I had two starting pitchers, I would want them to see who they would be facing in the regular season."

When Gene Mauch came to manage the Twins in 1976, he wanted to retain the number four. Steve Braun was wearing that number at the time, which posed a problem. I wouldn't follow Mauch's desire and switch numbers around, since I didn't feel that a manager should make a player give up his number. Howard Fox was mad at me for not giving into Mauch's demands, but I still wouldn't back down. Eventually, the problem was solved when Braun agreed to give up his number. I'm not sure if it had anything to do with the number crises, but Braun was playing in Seattle in 1977.

Camilo Pascual was a coach for the Twins and became involved in a dispute over his salary. Calvin and Camilo were having a difference of opinion over an extra one thousand dollars. Some people in the organization talked him into leaving, and he signed with Oakland.

Camilo is the scout that discovered Jose Canseco. It's possible that the Twins might have signed the powerful hitter if they could have struck a deal with Camilo. The difference was as small as one thousand dollars, which wouldn't have been much compared to Canseco's impact on the Twins.

Chapter 5

The Bat Boys

In 1961, the Twins' first year in Minnesota, I was instructed to fly to Minnesota because they were running a promotion to choose "Twin Bat Boys." (Incidentally, Calvin's brothers, Jimmy and Billy Robertson were also twins).

I flew to the Cities in the morning and returned later in the same day. I was reluctant to go since it was a very busy and hectic part of spring training. In addition, I didn't know the area very well. I had only been in the Twin Cities once before and then only for three days in the winter.

On my first trip to Minnesota, Doc Lentz and myself were in the Twin Cities to get acclimated to our new surroundings and see the stadium. We stayed at the Radisson Hotel in Minneapolis and were going to explore the town later that evening. Doc called me as I was looking out the window of my hotel room. Suddenly, I saw what looked like a person flying by the window. Doc disputed my claim, but when we got to the lobby the bell cap told us that a construction worker had fallen. This event helped form my first impression of Minnesota.

This time, my second trip, I arrived at Metropolitan

Stadium in March as 74 sets of twins sat patiently in the stands. The stadium had been used by the AAA Minneapolis Millers of the American Association for the past five years. The club wanted me to interview each pair of kids in one day and decide which pair would win the contest. I didn't look forward to the task.

Thankfully, a Twins scout, Angelo Giuliani, helped me pick out the bat boys. Angelo and I went into the Stadium Club, which was a restaurant and bar in the basement of the old Met to meet with each pair of twins. I had a particular set of questions to ask each set of kids before choosing a pair to work for the club. The first one was their age. The second asked their parents feelings about the prospect of them becoming bat boys. Their transportation to the stadium was the third concern. Another question inquired what school they attended. Finally, the last question asked where they lived.

Angelo would shake his head if the kids lived too far away from the stadium, because he had been in Minnesota longer than me. Driving an hour back and forth from the Met would have gotten old really fast for the kids' parents. We finally selected Peter and Richard King from Rosemount. I asked, "What type of work do you do now?"

They responded in unison. "We work on a farm."

I said, "What time do you wake up?"

"Five a.m."

Angelo and I looked at one another. Five in the morning was quite early. Of course, I was accustomed to waking up later and staying at the ballpark late.

"We wake up and do some chores," they continued. "We go to school and then come back home to do the rest of our chores."

I was surprised by the amount of work they were undertaking. "If you have all these chores to do, how can you work at the ball park?"

One of them said, "Our parents are going to let us stop working on the farm if we get this job."

It seemed like a fair response. I continued with the interrogation. "Have you ever played Little League ball?"

They answered, "No."

"Have you ever been to a ball game?"

Again, they said, "No."

I was impressed by these kids and the amount of hard work that they did. I also liked the fact that they didn't seem overly interested in baseball.

Half the kids I interviewed talked about hitting .300, which meant they would want to be with the players the entire time and wouldn't do any work. A bat boy has a tremendous amount of work to do every game for little pay, and it's not all fun. He would have to come at three in the afternoon until eleven or twelve at night. They had to pass out laundry, get the team balls signed, shine shoes, clean up, run errands for the players, and many other jobs. I hired the kids from the farm and they did a good job, but I decided I didn't want a contest like that again.

In the future I went out into the stands whenever necessary and picked out kids who became bat boys. I saw this guy that came to just about every game and I said, "How many games have you been to?"

Tommy Wescott answered, "Thirty-three."

"And how many times have you sneaked in?" I continued my questioning.

"Thirty three," he responded again.

I said, "I'm going to hire you since it's not going to cost the club any money in receipts."

He worked for me for three or four years until he entered the military. While in the Navy, stationed in Hawaii, Calvin treated him to a fifty-dollar-a-plate winter baseball meeting dinner. Much to the chagrin of Howard Fox, who thought that the president of the ball club should not have dinner with a lowly bat boy. But, that was Calvin Griffith.

Mark Stodghill was another bat boy who worked for me. He drove my car a grand total of two times. I was reluctant to let him drive more frequently, because each time he drove, he had an accident. The first time, he was on the parking lot of Metropolitan Stadium and hit a pole. He ripped off the side of the car. The second time was right before the 1965 All-Star Game.

Joe Cronin, Calvin's brother-in-law and then the president of the American League, decided to give the home and visiting clubhouse managers a gift. He also gave the bat boys a gift. I asked Cronin how he could give watches to the bat boys, but not the ball boys since they were both necessary for the game. He wasn't going to have any discussion on the matter. He simply stated, "Well, we are not giving them anything."

I was upset and staged a futile attempt to argue. "We have a ball boy down each foul line, another gives the balls to the umpire and two bat boys. You're going to give away two watches to five kids. What do you want us to do? Flip a coin? That's not fair."

He was unmoved by my desire and repeated

unemotionally, "Well, that's how we're going to do it."

A couple hours later I received a call from Howard Fox. He knew I was very upset about the ball boys being left out, but was smart enough not to mention it. He asked timidly, "Can you have someone take Joe Cronin to a Catholic Church?"

I went over to Mark Stodghill, our troubled driver, I said, "Would you mind driving Joe Cronin to St. Richard's Church in Richfield?"

Mark did as I asked. As he pulled into the parking lot he was hit by a car and tore up the back of my car again. It wasn't his fault, but he was very concerned about my reaction and turned white as a sheet. In addition, he was becoming known as a kid who couldn't drive well. It's better never to give a player something they could use to razz a person.

Joe Cronin looked nervous as he came into the locker room after church. "First, I want to tell you something. The kid got into an accident, but it wasn't his fault. He's outside in the hallway and he's afraid to come into the clubhouse."

I was obviously quite upset about my car getting smashed for the second time. "Where did you say he was?"

Cronin stated, "He's in the hallway. But, let me tell you something. It wasn't his fault. And one more thing, all the kids are getting watches." If the accident hadn't happened, the clubhouse kids probably never would have received a memento of the All-Star game.

I had a bat boy who did a great job for me one year, 1967, but then started screwing up a lot the next year. He seemed to be an entirely different person. There was a complete and total transformation. It got to be around August and I met with him and said, "Look, you're doing a lousy job this year, and I'm ready to let you go. But, since the season is almost over and we have a chance to make the playoffs and into the money, I'll let you stay for the rest of the season. After that, you're gone. Is that agreed?"

He quickly agreed to our arrangement and the club tied for second that season. In major league baseball if a team finished in the top three positions, the club is given money that is distributed to players and people within the team. Since the season was over, the kid left quickly. I hardly gave him another thought until the spring.

I received a message from Minnesota, during spring training. It said the same bat boy was planning on returning for the next season despite our agreement. I wrote the boy a letter, reminded him of our talk, and told him that I didn't want him to come back the next year.

A week after my letter was sent, I received a call from his mother who said that her son had been involved with drugs. His school work had slipped and he had gotten into some trouble with the law.

All of the bat boys had made a deal with their schools. If the boys did well in their classes, they were dismissed from school for day games. It was similar to a work-study program. The kid and his mother had made an agreement with the school to make up all the school work. If he caught up with his school work, he could still go to day games the next season. They made this agreement without taking into account that I didn't want the boy to work for me during the next Twins season. The mother cried on the phone and feared that her son's dismissal would cause him to go back into drugs.

I was still very reluctant to hire this kid again, but I agreed to give him a second chance. I told him, "Make sure you get plenty of sleep. If I see something in your eyes, or you look tired ... If I see anything strange about you ... I'm going to let you go immediately without any explanation. You're gone. You're history. So, you better get plenty of sleep."

He did a great job, but was afraid to even yawn. I was kind of proud of the decision I made regarding his second chance, and today he is a very successful businessman.

* * *

The father of a potential ball boy called me and wanted me to hire his son, Randy Segal. I never hired people's children or friends, I preferred to hire kids that hung around the stadium since they tended to work harder. If I hired a friend's son, the kid might screw around more. It is more difficult to fire the son of a friend. This kid's father called Jim Wiesner and talked him into hiring his son for the visiting clubhouse. I watched the kid work hard and hired him to work for the home team during the next season.

During one of the first few games, I got a call from Calvin. He had been watching the bat boy from his private box, and told me to tell Randy to get a haircut. Calvin wanted his employees to wear their hair in a short, professional manner. One year, he withheld my bonus check until I went in for a trim.

But, Randy's hair was really long and I told him to get it cut by the next homestand. I hadn't given it much thought until the team came back, and I noticed that he was always wearing a hat. I grabbed his hat from him and discovered that he never cut his hair, he merely hid it under his cap. I immediately let him go, but he returned the next day with short hair and I decided to give him another chance.

Soon after this, I heard that he had been telling his

parents that he had to work until one or two in the morning when he had left the stadium at eleven. I confronted him, "Do you know what would happen if the Child Labor people thought you were here until that hour in the morning. All the kids would immediately be let go and I don't think you want that to happen. I'll make a deal with you. I am going to give you enough time to get home from the stadium and then I'm going to call. The first night your not there when I call, you will be fired." He agreed to this and he was always there when I called.

About a week later, the usher told me that someone was in the hallway with a package for me. Jim Segal, Randy's dad, handed me a large bottle of liquor. "I want to thank you. I tried to get him to cut his hair, and to come in earlier, but he never would until you talked to him."

I handed the bottle back to him. "You don't need to give me this. The one thing that got him to do these things was his love for the job. I'm not his parent, he should be home because of you. Not me. Keep your bottle of booze. He's going to go by my rules while he's working here, or he's not going to work for me. And no parent, or anyone else is going to change that." Mr. Segal thanked me and left, his son worked for me for several years without any more problems.

* * *

Occasionally, I had problems with executives who criticized the kids I hired. Jimmy and Billy Robertson sat down the foul line during games and would discuss some of the ball boys. They would say that one didn't run well, or another couldn't throw far. The Robertsons thought that a bat boy also should be a good ballplayer.

I was bothered by their criticisms. I went to them and said, "I didn't hire them to be a ballplayer. It's your job to find the ballplayers! I hired them to work in the clubhouse, and they do a great job in the locker room."

Despite the Robertsons' wishes, I never hired bat boys on their ability to play baseball. My only requirement was that they gave me one hundred percent. And if their pluses outweighed their minuses I allowed them to work in the clubhouse, despite negative commentaries from outsiders.

Another set of identical twin bat boys, not from a contest, worked for me. Keith and Ken Carlson caused me a great degree of confusion when they first started working for me. Originally I only hired Keith to work as a bat boy, but Ken used to always hang around the stadium. One day, I told Keith to go up the umpire's room to clean up the lockers. I didn't give it a second thought, until I walked out into the hallway. I was very surprised to find the kid was just standing in the hall. I got really upset, as I did when the kids didn't follow instructions.

I said, "Didn't I tell you to go to the umpire's room? When I ask you to do something, I want you to do it."

The kid said nothing, turned around and walked away. I was still bothered by his lack of action, and I even considered firing him on the spot. I found out later that it was Ken, rather than the bat boy Keith, who was in the hallway. I thought I was going crazy, since I was seeing double. Instead of being confused all the time, I decided to hire Ken also. But, I still couldn't tell them apart. From then on, I would call to them "Ken-Keith" since I couldn't tell them apart.

Ken and Keith's mother sent me an article soon after the bat boys were hired. Much to my surprise, they had been featured in an article on April 20, 1961. I had hired them sixteen or seventeen years later, but the article had the two Carlsons' as babies. They had been the first set of identical twins born while the Twins were in Minnesota. In addition, they had been born on the Twins' first home game. It was quite an odd coincidence.

Mark McKenzie was another bat boy who provided me with a story. He was a student at the University of Minnesota, and he came down to Florida during spring training one year.

He didn't have much money and asked if he could stay in the clubhouse for a couple of nights. I agreed, but while he was there he suffered a ruptured appendix. Jim Wiesner was also staying in the clubhouse that night and they immediately called Dr. Leonard Michienzi. They took him to the hospital and he was in really rough shape throughout the night. The doctor and Wiesner tried to get in touch with the boy's parents and me.

To make matters worse, Mark didn't have any health insurance because he was not in school at the time. The people at the hospital were obviously concerned about the bill, but Calvin said not to worry about it. He said they had to take care of the boy and he guaranteed the bill would be paid. He was in the hospital for six or seven weeks and Calvin paid to fly Mark's mother to visit him. She stayed in a hotel for most of the time her son was in the hospital. Calvin paid for everything during her stay in Orlando, including meals in the hotel.

Mark's father eventually received medical coverage for his son through his employment, but Calvin still took care of their other expenses. Mark was just a guy, who wasn't even working for the club at the time and Calvin took very good care of him and his family.

Calvin often received calls from fathers and grandfathers

who wanted their sons to be bat boys. Calvin always said, "I don't have anything to do with the clubhouse. You'll have to work out a deal with Ray Crump. I'll never ask Raymond to hire anybody. He knows who he needs and who he wants."

This practice even worked for people high up the corporate totem pole. Jamie Lowe, whose grandfather, H. Gabriel Murphy, owned forty percent of the ball club before Calvin sold it, wanted to work in the clubhouse. He made a deal with Howard Fox, but Calvin said that they would find something else for the young man to do. Jamie eventually worked in the public relations department before becoming assistant to the Twins' president. But Calvin wouldn't interfere with my business. In all the years I worked for Calvin, he never told me who to hire. For this, I will always be thankful.

One of the benefits of being a bat boy was the opportunity to make a road trip each year, provided they did a good job. The greatest thrill for me as a bat boy was the road trip, and I think it is something the kids will never forget. Sometimes it was hard to convince the executives that the kids deserved to make a trip. I went to Howard Fox toward the end of one season with a list of the kids and the trips they wanted to take. Howard said, "I have made a decision. I don't think these kids should make a trip this year."

I walked away and began to think of what to tell the kids, since I knew they would be very disappointed. I decided to explain the situation to Calvin. He said, "No problem. I'll take care of it. What trip do you want them to go on?"

We took out a Twins' schedule and I pointed out an road trip. "How about this one?"

He said, "That's fine. Don't worry about a thing. You tell those kids that they can take a trip."

The next day, Calvin and Howard were up in the private box and watched a ball boy running down the line. Calvin asked, "What trip are they going to go on?"

Howard didn't say anything. Then Calvin pulled out a schedule and picked the same dates that we had earlier discussed and said, "I think this trip will be good." Howard didn't dare rebuff Calvin. Later, he said to me, "The boss says the kids can go on this trip." I couldn't believe that Fox would try to knock the poor kids out of one of the most rewarding and memorable trips of their lives.

One of the most tedious jobs in the life of a bat boy is cleaning cleats. Do I look like I'm having fun?

When I was a bat boy for Washington, I loved standing around the batting cage talking to Jackie Jensen & others.

Chapter 6

The Tenth Man

Calvin often called me "The Tenth Man." He thought that the entire team must work well together in order for it to be successful. The team included "the nine guys out on the field, and Ray Crump." He felt that I was an important aspect to the team.

After games I provided a buffet for the players. I started serving pizzas, if they won, and gradually went to roast beef sandwiches, hamburgers, chicken and other food. The most memorable snack, according to the players, were the cakes. My wife, Carol, baked them for the players whenever they celebrated a birthday and decorated them to reflect the interests of the players. If one of them played cards, she would place a full house or royal flush on the frosting. The players preferred Carol's cakes and would complain if I had the audacity to substitute one purchased in a store. Of course they didn't realize that her cakes came in a box with Pillsbury stamped on it.

Carol also made cakes to celebrate a special event in a player's career. Sometimes, the cake delivery predated the event it was supposed to commemorate. When Harmon Killebrew was vying for his 500th home run, she made a mammoth combination of flour, water and frosting to celebrate the occasion. It was decorated and ready for presentation, but he didn't scale the fence. At the start of every game, we would defrost the cake. When he didn't hit the home run, the cake returned to the freezer. We did this every day for quite a while until he finally hit the milestone.

A perk of being the Minnesota Twins equipment manager was the chance to drive a new club car every year. In the years I was with the ball club, a Ford dealership would give us cars. In fact, I received over thirty new cars in eleven years in exchange for player appearances.

On one particular occasion, I called the general manager of Bob Carter Ford, Herb Kessler, because I was having trouble with the air conditioning. When I called the dealership, the receptionist said that the general manager's mother had died. She also told me the name of the funeral parlor that was holding the visitation. At the time, my sons were very young and we were having friends from Florida visiting us. I told Carol that after the game I would go over to the funeral parlor and then come home since we had plans that evening.

When I arrived at the mortuary I asked, "Could you tell

me the room that Mrs. Kessler is being seen in?"

A solemn faced man in a black suit responded, "Mrs. Kessler is not being seen today."

I went into a monologue without hesitation, "What are you telling me? Do you realize that I came here all the way from Bloomington? [Bloomington was only seven miles away.] I went through all this traffic, in a car with no air conditioning when it's ninety degrees outside. And you're telling me I can't see her?"

The man was unmoved by my plight.

"No, you can't."

With a straight face, I said, "Well, do you have anybody else I can see?"

"No!" He shouted and ran into a back office. He looked startled, shocked and frightened. He was devoid of any sense of humor.

The next day, Carol and I went back to the funeral parlor. I had told my wife about the incident, but she didn't think it was very amusing.

The man from the previous day was standing in the hallway when we arrived. When he recognized me, he darted toward the back office. We thought the sudden transformation to a track star was odd. It's not every day where a funeral parlor director in a full three-piece suit runs down a quiet hallway. Carol and I proceeded up the stairs when the office door slowly opened up again and three heads popped through the slightly parted door.

One by one, each head appeared on top of the other until it formed a totem pole of horizontal heads. The men looked like "The Three Stooges." They had to think "The nut is back." Carol looked away from them embarrassed and quickly scampered up the stairs.

Oh well, I still think it was funny.

After night games, I often went downtown and ate at "The Tick-Tock." It was an all-night fast food restaurant, which featured the best bean soup in Minneapolis.

One night, two bus drivers entered the diner and argued about how many baseballs were used in a pro ball game. They also questioned the total amount of baseballs that teams had before the game started.

The first guy said "I know they start with one hundred."

The second driver said, "No, they start with sixty. I heard this Ray Crump say on a television program that they start with sixty."

The first man wouldn't believe that they used only sixty

baseballs per game. To make things more interesting, they bet five dollars on the outcome of their disagreement. I figured they would go out to the next Twins game and count each ball that was thrown in the game. I was mistaken.

After the bet was made, the drivers agreed to call me when they went to work the next day at 4:00 p.m. The whole time I had just been sitting next to them enjoying my bean soup. I withheld the temptation to say anything to the men.

The next day, at five minutes to four, the phone rang. I picked it up and said simply, "We use sixty baseballs."

You should have heard them arguing on the phone. One guy accused the other of calling ahead of time, and he denied it. I hung up and let them discuss my answer.

I often played tricks on Doc Lentz, the Twins' former trainer. He was the kind of guy who didn't like to spend much money.

The trainer went downtown a few times to be on "The Halsey Hall Show." Halsey Hall, who was the broadcaster for the Twins when we came to Minnesota, used to do a television show that would come on before every televised Twins' game. He would be asked questions on the air and if he couldn't answer it, you would win a gift from Twin City Luggage. Each time, Lentz paid fifteen to twenty dollar to a cabbie to take him to the city for the show.

I wanted to see Doc's reaction to missing out on a free gift. "Ya know, you should get a gift for going down there. Every time I do his show, I get a gift."

"No, you don't get a gift. I've done the show several times, but never received anything."

I kept assuring him that I received a gift each time I appeared. Prior to the show, an announcer would tell who was trying to stump Halsey Hall on the show, and what they would win.

I continued my assurance that he should have been getting his gifts. I added that if he didn't pick up his present, Halsey Hall would be given the gift certificates and he used them for Christmas presents. Doc started to agree. "You mean I've been taking a cab there and a cab back, and I could have been getting gifts."

"Definitely," I reiterated what I said. "You could have had a complete set of luggage by now for your whole family."

"Well, I'll be damned."

I finally had him.

Doc went into the dining room to get a couple of drinks, after a game, when he ran into Halsey Hall.

Halsey said, "Doc, I want you to come back on my show."

"Well, if I come on your show, what kind of gifts do I get?" Doc was through fooling around. He wanted to lay things on the line.

"Well Doc," Halsey responded, "I don't give gifts on my show."

Doc had already seen on television that all gifts were provided by Twin City Luggage.

Halsey continued, "What you get is prestige for coming on my show."

"Oh yea," an infuriated Doc said. "Take that prestige and stick it up your ass. I'm not coming on your show."

Halsey Hall stood there in silence. He couldn't understand what had just transpired. Doc who passed away, the poor soul, never realized that I was just kidding about the gifts.

I also played a "shoe repair" trick on Doc. We sent the ball players' shoes over to St. Paul to be repaired. Jim Wiesner, the visiting clubhouse manager, took the shoes to the repair shop. When he came back with the repaired shoes, he would give me the bill and I reimbursed him for the expense. Doc Lentz, who I've already mentioned was kind of frugal with his money, gave a pair of shoes to Wiesner to get repaired. After

Jim came back with Doc's shoes, he gave him the bill for $12.50. Doc thought that was kind of high since he just got half soles on them, it being the sixties and all, and asked me what I thought.

Actually, Doc thought Wiesner was making money off the shoe repair. Of course, I didn't discourage his belief. I feigned ignorance and told Doc that I wasn't sure if he was making any money off it.

I called Ernie Pesis, a friend of mine who owned a bar in Minneapolis, and asked him if he wanted to have a little fun with Doc. He quickly agreed, and I explained he would receive a call from Doc asking for Joe's Shoe Repair. Doc was going to ask how much it would cost to repair his shoes, and Ernie was to say $7.50. I went back to Doc Lentz, "Upon careful reconsideration I have determined that the price may be kind of steep."

He said, "Well, I know it's high. I can't believe that after all the things I've done for Jim Wiesner, he goes and makes money off me. I mean he has to take the spikes over there anyway. Why can't he just take my shoes along without making a profit?"

I quickly arrived at a solution. "Why don't you do this? I just looked up the number; it's 333-8907. Call Joe's Shoe

Repair and ask them how much it would cost."

So Doc took the bait, and made the phone call. Ernie picked up the phone and said, "Joe's Shoe Repair, how may I help you?"

Doc said, "Let me ask you a question. How much would it cost to half sole a pair of shoes?"

"Seven-fifty," responded Ernie.

"Seven-fifty? Doc's blood pressure was rising. "You don't charge any more than seven-fifty?"

"Nope," Ernie said, "I've never charged anyone more than seven-fifty in my life."

Doc got off the phone and wasn't happy. He ran into Jim a couple days later.

"You son-of-a-bitch," Doc steamed, "I can't believe you made money off me. I'm never going to give you my shoes to get repaired again." Wiesner didn't know what to say. In addition, he wasn't sure why Doc was so fumed. Jim looked dumbfounded, a look Doc must have been getting used to by now.

Another joke we played on various ballplayers involved "Auto-Foolers." These were firecrackers that were connected to the car. When the car was started, smoke and loud pops were seen and heard from the engine.

We played this joke on some Cuban ballplayers and all four doors of the car opened in unison. The players ran from the car and dove to the ground. They took it as a very real threat to their life--as though Fidel Castro was after them.

Halsey Hall was on the plane with the club when we took off from LaGuardia in New York. Halsey was never very comfortable when flying. He used to wrap a pillow around his head whenever we were taking off or landing. When the plane got up into the air, the pilot encountered engine trouble. In addition, the landing gear wouldn't go down properly. We were forced to land again in Newark, New Jersey amidst ambulances, fire engines, and other emergency vehicles. We landed safely and everyone got off the plane, but Halsey was so upset he got off the plane and pissed on the runway.

Bob Wolff was a broadcaster who moved up to Minnesota from Washington with the team. One of the things I remembered most about him was a boy that used to cling to his side. The boy acted as his "caddy" and would carry his brief case and gifts for pregame show guests and perform other menial tasks. The "caddy" later became known to the country as

Maury Povich, the same guy with a morning talk show. I always remembered him, and think it's comical when he says now that he was a bat boy for the Washington Senators at the same time I worked there. I never saw him cleaning mud off cleats, or in any of the team photos.

Luis Tiant asked me to get him an advance on his check so he could send five hundred dollars home to his wife. He was given the advance and I sent John Harris, who worked with me in the locker room in Florida for many years, over to the bank to get a cashier's check. When he got back and gave me the check, I discovered he purchased a five hundred dollar War Bond instead of the check.

I called the bank to tell them the problem, but they said we needed to hold the bond for the ninety days. I used five hundred dollars from my personal checking account and sent John back to the bank with more explicit directions. He received the cashier's check and I kept the War Bond. After the ninety days were up, I went to cash the Bond and a new problem emerged. I wasn't allowed to cash the bond since it was in Tiant's name. Thus, I had to contact Tiant, who was just released from the club. I sent the check to Richmond, Virginia, where he was playing for the AAA Yankees, and I was finally able to get the Bond cashed.

After the end of the 1967 baseball season, Zoilo Versalles happened to mention that he planned on asking Calvin Griffith for an advance on the next year's salary. I said, "Zoilo, you might want to wait a little before you talk to Calvin."

Versalles had just lost the Twins an opportunity to make it into the playoffs by "Show-boating." A lazy ball was hit to him and he tried to make it look like a difficult catch. He missed it and a run score and we were out of the playoffs.

Zoilo ignored my advice and approached Calvin in his office. Calvin looked astonished that he would even come close to him after what had occurred. After the ballplayer made his request, Calvin turned and said, "Zoilo, you make me want to vomit!"

Zoilo didn't get his advance.

John Harris provided me with another amusing story of life behind the scenes in baseball. We were sitting in the clubhouse Saturday, and the cleaners were closed Sunday. It was always important to make sure we had plenty of towels for the weekend, since players often liked to dry themselves after showering. I asked John how many towels we had and he said,

"We have five hundred."

I said, "Good, that'll be plenty." I was confident that we had enough towels to last until Monday.

The next day I went to get the towels to lay throughout the locker room, but there were only nineteen. I went looking for John and asked him the whereabouts of the rest of the towels. He confidently responded, "They're at the cleaners."

"What?" I bellowed. "Yesterday when I asked you, you said we have five hundred."

He looked at me and said, "That's right. We have nineteen here and the rest are at the cleaners."

Anytime we went to another country, we were required to take the equipment through customs at the airport. Usually, I would have to go with the officials as they checked each team equipment bag. Meanwhile, all the players had to stand by their individual bags to have them searched. After our equipment was checked, we would put it on a truck and have it brought to the hotel. When I went to Canada, I would have a dozen autographed balls stuck under my arm. I would give the balls to the head of customs, who would distribute them to his employees and wave us through the gates. This saved us many hours of inspection time each trip, as well as much aggravation.

This worked most of the time, except after customs officers found drugs in the bag of Ferguson Jenkins' bags. The future Hall of Fame pitcher played for Texas at the time. The Twins, unfortunately, were the next team to arrive in Toronto. Thus, we had to pay the price for one player's mistake. I received an anonymous phone call, which stated all our bags would be checked at the customs office. There would be absolutely no exceptions. I was concerned that a player would try to sneak codeine tablets or something else out of the country. My fears were undaunted. It was no big deal and we didn't have a problem, but it's strange how one player can wreak havoc on the traveling of every other team in the league.

We had another problem with customs on an exhibition trip to Venezuela. We were told that teams wouldn't have to go through customs if they were on a charter flight. I bought some liquor while we were in the country, and I threw it in my bag before we left. When we got to the airport, the customs' agents announced that they were going to search through three bags. They believed if the random sample of three bags found nothing, then the rest of the bags would be okay.

I wasn't sure if my liquor was illegal, but I was nervous about the prospect and hoped they didn't check my bag. Well, they picked one bag, then another and found nothing in them.

Then, they grabbed my bag and I was even more concerned about it. I said to Doc Lentz, in a voice loud enough for the customs people to hear, "I hope they don't check number fifteen's bag. If anyone has anything it's him." (The players all had numbers on their bags. Number fifteen belonged to Al Worthington.)

They dropped my bag and picked up Al's. This bag belonged to the cleanest guy on the whole team. He didn't drink, smoke, or do drugs. Al had been a big drinker earlier in his career, but was completely sober by this trip. Thus, I was sure that he wouldn't have anything in his bag. The agents searched it very carefully from top to bottom, found nothing, and let us go on our way.

On another trip to Toronto, we had a lousy flight across the border and I asked the inspector if he would just let us pass. He reluctantly agreed, and I rode in the truck with the equipment and went to the hotel. The rest of the team was waiting with their personal bags. Howard Fox was looking for me, but I had already left the airport. Gene Mauch, the manager, said, "If it was a player, an executive, a reporter, or anyone else with this organization, I would worry about him. But, you don't have to worry about Ray Crump. He can take care of himself. In fact, he's probably sitting at the hotel with our bags right now."

Howard Fox wouldn't believe it. He said, "No way. He had to wait with the equipment. There's no way he is at the hotel."

The team left the airport and when they arrived at the hotel, I was sitting in the lobby. Mauch just shook his head and said, "You don't need to worry about Ray Crump." Fox stormed off to the bar.

A sad thing happened to us during spring training one year. It is something that most people never hear about, but it does happen. We had a trunk in Orlando where we kept valuables. Every week the players would get their checks for meal money and other expenses. Many ball players would endorse their check for either me or an assistant to get cashed for them. All the cash for the checks would be placed in individual envelopes, which we would put in the valuable box. We had a player that we thought was stealing money from this box.

Once, after returning with the envelopes, Howard Fox and myself waited in the bathroom. We watched this player go into Rod Carew's box and take the envelope. The thief chose Rod Carew, since obviously he was the star of the team. He was making the most money, and he had special privileges. He was the only player who had a private bat room. Since, people were stealing his valuable bats, we had to keep them separate from the rest. We didn't tell Carew or anyone else about the incident with the former player, but we did confront him. Soon after this solemn occasion, he was traded. These events are rare, but they do happen. Sometimes a person's performance on the field is not the only reason they are released from a team.

Most people do not give the baseballs much thought, but they are integral to the game. The baseballs used in a major league game, contrary to public opinion, are not completely white. They are rubbed with a special mud from Pennsauken Creek in New Jersey. A former player named Lena Blackburne collected the mud about a mile from his home, put it in a coffee can, and sold it to the club for fifty dollars a can. The umpires would rub mud onto sixty of these balls per game, and if they ran out the equipment manager would "ready" some more baseballs.

There used to be many fines levied on players by each other for various offenses. Players would be fined if they were late, made an error, walked too many opposing players, didn't hustle, and that type of things. A court was set up for people who considered their fine unjust. However, if you lost in this "kangaroo court" then the fine was increased. After the season, the players would hold a big party with the money gained from these fines.

In late September or early October, a big party was held at Duffy's in Minneapolis. Duffy's was owned by Joe Duffy, who was the first director of Stadium Operations at the Met. We all went to that bar in 1963, and all the drinks were seventy-five cents to a dollar, and Duffy said he would take care of our food, but we had to pay for our drinks. The jar was stuffed to the rim with over eleven hundred dollars to pay for drinks for 32 people. When I went to the party, I parked on the fifth floor of Dayton's parking lot.

Although I only had alcohol on rare events, I freely indulged this evening. The players were quite amused at this uncharacteristic display and kept bringing me screwdrivers. When we were finally ready to leave, the players started to wager on how far I could drive down the parking lot ramp before crashing my car into a wall. The ramp was one of those circular ones, which made it even more difficult to maneuver. The ramp was dangerous even for the best and most sober drivers.

Harmon Killebrew took pity on me and my condition. He told the other players to stall me while he went to get his car.

I said, "The heck with this I'm going to get my car."

Wally Post, who had just joined the club from the Reds grabbed me and threw me in Killebrew's car when it arrived. They drove me to my apartment and made sure I was in safely before leaving. After they left, I ran downstairs hailed a cab and went back to retrieve my car. I wasn't going to let players tell me when I had to go home. And, I wasn't going to let them tell me that I couldn't drive when I wanted.

By the grace of God, I made it home alive with no dents in the car and without injuring anyone else. It was a stupid thing to do, but I was soon back in my apartment. Then, the bed started to spin. It was the first time I had ever been drunk in my life. The next thing I knew, I ran into the bathroom and vomited. If I would have had a gun, I would have shot myself in the head to ease my pain. I knew there was no way I could live through that night.

The next day, I drove to work and I still felt like a train had run me over several times when I saw Calvin Griffith. I ducked down between two cars so he wouldn't see me in my deteriorated condition. I stumbled into the training room as the players were preparing for a game. I laid down on the table and some players would come into the room and whisper, "Shhh, Shhh! Come on, be quiet. Ray's sleeping." After my recovery,

I vowed never to drink again.

When Minnesota and New York used to match up at Metropolitan Stadium in the sixties, the place was always packed. Of course, it helped that the Yankees had been in the past five World Series (1960-1964) and had dominated most of the fifties. Our game was rained out one day, and Calvin wanted to play a day and a night game. Thus, the teams could divide the receipts from two games, rather than a double-header. Johnny Blanchard played for the Yanks and was their player representative. He was bothered by the two game format. He referred to me as "Calvin's righthand man" and made some negative comments about Calvin while I was in the visitor's clubhouse.

"That cheap ass Calvin Griffith," Blanchard exclaimed. "That cheap son-of-a-bitch has us playing two games."

Calvin found out about this, and I confirmed what he had heard. Later in his career, Blanchard tried to hook onto the Twins in some capacity since he was born in Minneapolis. Calvin was not interested. It just goes to prove that when you say bad things about good people, it comes back at you.

The St. Paul police force and the Minneapolis police

used to play a charity game against each other every year at Metropolitan Stadium. I would work these games and supply the toiletries, towels, and baseballs. One day, right before the game, I was pulled over with three other cars for speeding. I said to the Minneapolis police officer, "I don't want you to take this as a threat or a bribe, but if you give me a ticket, you can supply your own soap, towels and baseballs."

The officer took my license back to his car and returned a few minutes later and let me go, but ticketed the other drivers. The next day, I saw the same officer playing first base. He glanced at me, smiled, and returned to the game.

When the Vikings played in Metropolitan Stadium, they used the same dressing room as the Twins. I would have to move the Twins equipment out of the clubhouse before they played, which obviously became a major pain. At the time, the Vikings would stay at the Marriot in Bloomington on the night before the game. In the hotel, they would tape their wrists and hands, and thus didn't need the training room. So I made a deal with the general manager of the Vikings, Jim Finks, and the trainer to move the tables from the training room and put them in the main locker room. This way I could move the Twins' equipment into the training room instead of moving it outside the clubhouse and then move it back.

When the Vikings came for a game, the coach, Norm Van Brocklin, didn't like the new set up. He said, "Hey, we're not going to have this set up like this. We want the training room."

I said, "What do you mean, I have been here since seven this morning setting up this. We made an agreement."

He wouldn't listen. He said, "Where's Billy Robertson? I want to see Billy Robertson."

I retorted, "When I want something, I go to the top. Don't you want to go to the top? Let's go see Calvin Griffith."

He agreed and the trainer, Brocklin and I went up to see Calvin. While in his office, we argued back and forth until Calvin interjected. Calvin said, "Raymond, now you be quiet for a moment. Let's hear what they have to say."

Brocklin said, "We have the rights to the locker room. We don't want the player's tables out in the locker room. We want the training room. We want everything moved out."

Then Calvin said, "Now Raymond, Let's hear your side of the story." I told him about the meeting and the rest of the story. He said, "Is that right?"

The trainer nodded his head.

"Well, a deal's a deal," Calvin said.

Brocklin shouted, "I don't care if a deal was made! We're using that training room! Do you want me to go tell Max Winter (Vikings President) that we can't use the training room?"

Now, Calvin was mad. He got up and in a loud voice said, "Let me tell you something. When you go back to Max Winter, you tell him that it came from the horse's mouth. You're not using the training room!" This was just one of several times that Calvin backed me up.

Jimmy Robertson, Calvin's brother, used to be close friends with the owner of Foremost Ice Cream. They ran advertisements in the stadium score book that said, "All ice cream in the stadium from the fans to the players is Foremost Ice Cream."

When I came into work one morning, the ice cream freezer was missing. I walked down to concessions and was told that Robertson had it removed. The Foremost Company felt they could sell more ice cream by using the freezer upstairs. While I sold ice cream to twenty or thirty guys, they could sell to an entire stadium.

I wasn't happy with the decision at all, and decided to switch ice cream companies. I chose Franklin Dairy, which had been sponsoring Harmon Killebrew. I made a deal with the company to switch if they could have a freezer with ice cream delivered within an hour.

Jimmy Robertson found out about the switch and was very upset. He ran to Calvin's office, but the president was on a golf course. When Mr. Griffith returned to the office, Jimmy told him about the ice cream.

Calvin said, "I don't want to hear a god damned thing about the ice cream. That's Raymond's clubhouse and he has the rights to the concessions in the locker room. That's your problem. You went and had the freezer taken out so it's your tough luck. If they can't provide enough freezers for the entire stadium then I'm not worried about them. And I don't have a god damn thing to do with the clubhouse. It's Raymond's and he can have whatever type of ice cream he wants." Again, Calvin backed up a decision that I made.

Salesmen often came to me in an attempt to persuade the club to buy their products. When I turned them down, often they would make an appointment to see Calvin. When the meeting took place, Calvin would always tell them, "Look, I'm the president of the ball club. I don't run the clubhouse, or have anything to do with it. If you can work out a deal with Raymond Crump, then the deal's set. Then, and only then will you be doing equipment business with this ball club."

Billy Robertson had a set of keys for all the rooms in Metropolitan Stadium. He approached me and said that he had lost all the keys. I immediately called the Bloomington Locksmith Office and hired them to change the locks in the locker room, umpires' room, and equipment rooms.

Billy came walking down the hall as the locksmith was in the hallway changing locks and said, "Who hired you to do this?"

The man replied, "Ray Crump."

Robertson said, "Well change them back. I want all the original locks back on the doors."

I came back down the hallway, and was surprised the locksmith was just about done.

"You're working fast," I said.

He responded dejectedly, "I haven't changed a thing."

I looked at him and said, "What do you mean? You haven't changed the locks?"

"No," he said. "I haven't, Billy Robertson told me to stop."

I immediately went to the private booth, since the Twins were playing a day game. I said sternly to Calvin, "I'm not going to be responsible for the clubhouse. Billy lost the keys to the locker room, and I'm not going to be held responsible for the players' equipment. And, I'm going to tell the players that I'm not responsible for their equipment!"

I had to make sure to tell Calvin about not being responsible for the players' personal items. Normally if a glove or personal other item is missing, they come howling to me.

Calvin said seriously, "Wait a minute. Who told them not to change the locks?"

I responded, "Billy."

He started to get irritated. "Well, where is he now?"

"Left field." He watched the games from the bleachers in left.

"How can we get a hold of him?"

I said, "We can call down to the grounds crew and they will get him."

When Billy got on the phone, Calvin stated, "God damn! We're not going to be responsible for all that equipment! You let that locksmith change those locks, and I don't want to hear a god damn thing about it!"

The locks were changed quickly without additional commentary.

On another occasion, I was working for the Minnesota

Kicks soccer team. I was hired to run their locker room on home games. I had to move the Twins' equipment in and out of the locker room as I did for the Vikings. We made an agreement that they would pay me a set amount of dollars for the job. I worked a few games with them, and I got paid for it.

Their head coach was Freddie Goodwin. He knew I didn't care anything about soccer. After a couple of games, the team was practicing and he asked, "Ray, what do you think about soccer now?"

At the other end of the field, the sprinklers were watering the grass. I said, "Freddie, let me tell you something. I think watching those sprinklers go back and forth is more exciting then watching soccer."

He looked at me and laughed, but I was serious.

After a while, the Kicks decided that they didn't want to pay me for working the games. They wanted to hire another equipment guy, and pay him a lot less money. Meanwhile, I would still have to move boxes of equipment out before the games and then return it. Well, hiring another equipment man was not the agreement they made with the club when they first came to the stadium.

The time came for a game, and I wouldn't let the Kicks in the locker room. The soccer team contacted Clark Griffith,

Calvin's son. He found me in the clubhouse and said, "You have to let them in the locker room."

I responded angrily, "No I don't."

Billy Robertson said "You can't keep them out."

I ignored him. The coach, Clark, and Billy went to Calvin in a huff.

Calvin immediately took my side of the argument. He said, "You can use that clubhouse when you pay Ray Crump the money you agreed to."

Billy and Clark were very upset about it, the coach handed me the cash, and I opened the clubhouse. After that, I was paid as was agreed upon by the now defunct Kicks.

The Twins trainer, Doc Lentz became sick during a season one year and I had to be the trainer and equipment manager for part of a road trip. A few days later, the Twins hired Buck Chamberlin to be the trainer. When Doc Lentz was better, he returned to the job and Chamberlin was sent to the minor league system. The Twins became concerned with Doc Lentz's health and hired a minor league trainer, Dick Martin, to be an assistant in case Lentz became ill. The club decided to go with Martin since he was much younger than Chamberlin.

Lentz became concerned about his job, and wouldn't let

Martin do anything important. Doc thought that Martin would immediately take over his job since he was younger and would work for less. Once the season was over, Dick Martin went to Venezuela. He had asked Howard Fox three times to be put on the pension plan which included medical. Martin wanted to drop his regular health insurance before he left for South America. Fox agreed to put him on the plan and Martin canceled his insurance.

While in Venezuela, Martin became very ill with meningitis and acquired a bill for $5,500, which he sent to the Twins. Howard had not put Martin on the plan as promised, and devised a plan to get rid of him. I walked by the conference room when Fox, Dr. Harvey O'Phelan and Dr. Leonard Michienzi were discussing Martin's dismissal and replacement.

Immediately, I went to Calvin and said, "You know they are planning on getting rid of Dick Martin. It's not fair at all, Doc Lentz didn't let him do anything and he has the potential to be a great trainer some day. He hasn't had a shot. If you get rid of Dick Martin, it's a rip off."

Calvin responded seriously, "Do you really think so?"

"There's no doubt in my mind."

Calvin said that he would take care of it. He walked into the meeting and said, "You know, I've had second thoughts on this and I've talked to Raymond who said that Martin didn't get a fair shake. So, we're going to give him another chance and we'll have a meeting like this next year." Thus, Dick Martin became the Twins trainer and has done a fabulous job.

In 1965, I was asked by Fox to get each player's correct ring size. I wrote on a sheet of paper the ring sizes for the players, myself, Jim Wiesner who ran the visitor's clubhouse, and Michienzi and O'Phelan, the team doctors. When I gave the list to Fox, he crossed Wiesner's name off. He said, "I think the first time you're in a World Series, you should limit the people who get rings."

This was a load of bullshit. Wiesner deserved the ring much more than other people who were on the list. He worked for the club full time and was there almost as often as I. But, Fox was in charge and I didn't know what I could do to help.

Wiesner overheard rumors that he was not on the list, and asked player representative Bob Allison. Jim told Bob that he wanted to get a ring and would even be willing to pay for it. Allison said that there was nothing that could be done.

I think that Wiesner was much more deserving than the team doctors. One of the doctors told my wife that he viewed his position with the club as a "hobby." He probably enjoyed the perks associated with the team. I figured out a way that I thought would get Wiesner a ring. I crossed my name off the list and wrote "Give my ring to Jim Wiesner."

Calvin saw this and called me into his office to ask me why I scratched my name off the list. I told him the story, but he really didn't say too much. I think he was trying to find out a way to rectify the situation.

On Christmas Day, my wife and I were celebrating our first Christmas together when there was a knock on the door. A special courier had delivered my World Series ring. It was beautiful. A full carat diamond surrounded with gold, my name, and '65 American League Champs.

In addition, Calvin gave one to Wiesner saying "Ray felt he was deserving of a ring, and would have given his up for him." To this day, Jim still doesn't know the story of how he got the ring.

On another occasion, Jim went to Fox and asked if he could make a road trip. Fox said, "You know, the person in charge of you is Ray Crump. You talk to him and if he decides that you should make a trip, then we will make arrangements."

I'm still not sure why Fox acted in this manner. Maybe he was hoping that I would choose to deny his trip. I thought the whole thing was kind of funny, since I thought he should make a trip the whole time. We decided that Wiesner should take a trip to New York and Boston. Fox didn't give it a second thought. He allowed the trip.

Now, Wiesner had a little problem. When he started to drink, he wanted to fight. He would bring up a grudge from ten years ago. A grudge that he never mentioned before and one that was forgotten by most. Wiesner was drunk in the hotel bar in Boston, when Howard came in with some friends. He and Fox exchanged some unpleasantries and began to scuffle. The fight was broken up by Harmon Killebrew and Bob Allison had to pull Jim off Fox. They dragged him to his hotel room to calm down, but he went back down to the bar after they had left and searched for Fox. Fortunately, Fox had already left the bar.

After this incident, Fox told me that he wanted me to find a reason to fire Wiesner. I told him that I didn't have any reason to fire him. After that, Fox tried to blame things on Wiesner so that he could fire him. Each excuse that Fox found was more absurd than the last. He even went so far as to blame Jim for the flat tire on the team station wagon. Eventually, Wiesner would have revenge.

Wiesner was the home team equipment manager since I left to start my own business. Actually, Jim Dunn (my assistant) was the first equipment manager when I left. Wiesner went to the front office in 1985 to knock Dunn out of position and become the home team clubhouse manager. The Twins were in contention to win the pennant and Wiesner wanted to make sure he received a full World Series share. But, Pohlad wouldn't let the Twins win with a team Calvin had built. Wiesner obtained the job of the Twins equipment manager and Dunn was delegated the responsibility of the visitor's locker room. Of course, now I am amused when I read articles or listen to Twins' broadcasts which refer to Jim Wiesner as the "Twins long-time clubhouse manager."

Several years later, after Calvin sold the team, Fox went to ask Jim's advice. Fox wanted to know if Ray Miller, who now is currently Pittsburgh's pitching coach, would make a good manager. Wiesner thought it was a crazy idea, but he said enthusiastically "I think Miller would make a great manager."

He thought that if Miller happened to win with the ball club, he would look like a genius. If the team played horrible, they would fire both Miller and Fox. As Jim saw it, he had nothing to lose. Miller had a horrendous time with the Twins. In 1985, the team was 50-50 while he was managing. The next year, the team was 59-80 and both Miller and Fox were fired.

The winter baseball meetings were held in Honolulu, Hawaii one year. I asked Calvin if Laurel Prieb, who worked in the public relations department, could go to the conference. I also thought that Laurel, currently an executive with the Milwaukee Brewers, was one of the hardest working people in baseball. He lived, breathed, and dreamed baseball. He was constantly working on the intricacies of baseball from early morning to late at night.

Calvin agreed to my request and Laurel made his first trip to Hawaii. On the return flight on a DC-10, I had to sit next to a very large woman on a plane cramped with baseball executives and families. Every time Laurel walked down the aisle, he smiled at my predicament.

I just had to get back at him. I told him that the woman was Aunt Jemima of the famous pancake mix. He wouldn't believe me, until I went to the store and purchased a box of her namesake. I gave it to Laurel as a present and said that she had sent me cases and cases of the stuff and I couldn't possibly ever use it all. To this day, Laurel still believes that woman was Aunt Jemima. In this case, I am the last one smiling.

Chapter 7

Antagonistic Relationships

During the years I was with the baseball organization, I had some less than friendly relationships. Some of them were temporary, such as players who were with the team a short time. Others, unfortunately, lasted longer. Regardless, many of them were memorable.

Joe Soucheray, a writer for the *Minneapolis Tribune*, was researching a story about the umpires strike. During the strike, the league had hired some "scab" labor to work the games while they were negotiating. The regular union umpires weren't very happy about the new umpires and had put up signs and covered the umpires' locker room with toilet tissue. Soucheray wanted to go into the room to take pictures of the newly "defaced" lockers. I told him that he didn't have a right to be in there without the umpires present.

He went to the room despite my wishes and knocked on the door. A bat boy happened to be in the room shining shoes. Soucheray told the boy that I had said it was okay to come in and take pictures, so the kid let him. When I found out about this, I went crazy and went looking for Soucheray. I checked the clubhouse, the dugout and finally found him coming out of the Twins offices. I grabbed him, threw him up against a wall, and told him that if he ever did something like that again, "I would beat his brains in." It's sad that something like that could occur, he violated the rights of the new umpires.

Later, we were able to put this behind us and become friends.

Bob Fowler, of the *St. Paul Dispatch*, was sneaking around the corner of the locker room one day looking for a "scoop." I saw his shadow and decided to play a joke and teach him a lesson for sneaking around the locker room. I told Jim Wiesner to go pack Rich Reese's bags. There were many rumors being spread, at the time, that he was going to be traded to Cleveland. The rumor was that Reese wanted out of Minnesota and Tony Horton wanted out of Cleveland. Many people in the area thought the two teams would swap players. After Fowler overheard what I told Wiesner, he ran out of the clubhouse.

When he found Tom Mee, the public relations director, he asked what the deal was with Reese. Tom told him that they were not going to say anything until 3:00 p.m. This writer took off toward the phone, and told the paper the story of the trade.

Later in the day, Fowler found Calvin Griffith and asked

what he felt about Reese being traded. Calvin looked confused. "Traded? We signed him."

Fowler was frazzled. "What do you mean you signed him? You traded him, didn't you?"

Calvin said again, "No, we signed him."

Fowler ran out of the office and called the paper back to get them to stop the story. He talked to his editor, Arno Goethel, who told him that it was too late.

"Where did you get your information?" Goethel asked.

"Well, Ray Crump told Jim Wiesner to pack Reese's bags," he said.

"Man, you've been had. Ray was playing a trick on you, and if I would have known you found out from him, I wouldn't have run the story."

The day after the story ran, Fowler wrote an article with the byline, "I was had." In the article, he called himself a "rookie" writer. Now, Fowler owns a minor league baseball team.

Another writer that I had an occasional problem with was Sid Hartman of the *Minneapolis Star Tribune*. I didn't like how he acted one way in front of the players, but acted differently when they were on a road trip. Whenever the players, coaches,

191

and managers were in town, Sid would compliment them and tell the guys how good they were in their last game. When the team was on the road, he would criticize them if they played poorly.

Sid had a radio show on Sundays, and he would constantly rip the players when they were out of town. The personnel was not oblivious to these criticisms, eventually it would get back to them. In July, 1993, Tom Kelly had a highly publicized sparring match over the radio with Sid Hartman. Apparently, Sid had criticized Dick Such, the pitching coach, and the Twins pitcher, Jim Deshaies. During the WCCO program, Kelly made Hartman aware that he was aware of the comments that were made before Kelly slammed down the phone.

When I was the equipment manager, I would tape these shows, and splice all Sid's criticisms together. When the players came back, they had a team meeting and after the meeting I played the tape for them. Sid was in the room when the tape began to play, and he couldn't believe what he was hearing. The tape had Sid criticizing a bunch of players on the team, saying this one should go to the minors, this one should be traded, and that type of thing. Sid was incensed. He shouted, "I'll get you fired! I'll get you fired! I'm going to Calvin." All the players laughed hysterically as Sid ran out of the room.

Sid is a real front-runner for sure, but he is a very hard working sports writer. He studies the sports writers in other cities and often cites them in his column. He often called my home in unsuccessful attempts to verify rumors. He would try to get more information from Carol.

Sid knew he was coming to an informed source, since my wife sewed on the jerseys for the club. Carol was one of the very first people to learn of a trade. As soon as I found out about a trade, I would call the equipment manager in that town and ask what size the player wore and then I would bring the jersey home to Carol.

Arno Goethel wrote for the *St. Paul Pioneer Press* and treated the players the same way as Sid Hartman. When the team was away, he would write bad things about the players and when they returned, he did the opposite. I had about 200 pens made up inscribed, "Poison Pen Goethel." I passed these pens out to everyone in the press box and broadcast booth. Everyone reacted much the way the players did in the locker room after the "Sid-Tapes." They all broke out laughing and Goethel turned bright red and left the press box.

* * *

In 1965, when I lived in Bloomington with Dave Boswell, the Twins pitcher from 1964-1970. Bill Hengen, a sports writer in Minneapolis, wrote an extremely critical article on Boswell's pitching. Boswell was really mad about the article and threatened, "If I see that guy, I'll punch him in the mouth."

The next day he pitched at Metropolitan Stadium. He was in the game for only three innings when he was pulled. When Boswell walked up the runway, he saw the reporter coming down the hallway looking for him. The dejected pitcher turned away from the locker room and slowly walked toward the outfield and Hengen followed. Boswell was leading him to a secluded area in right field. I ran after him because I knew when he got down there, he was going make good on his promise.

There was a large metal gate that separated the area where Boswell and Hengen were walking. I closed and locked the gate to separate the two. Hengen went crazy. "Let me in! Let me in!" He pleaded.

Hengen immediately ran to Calvin's box to complain. He whined, "Calvin your clubhouse guy locked me out. He doesn't have the right to keep the reporters away from a player."

Calvin didn't pay any attention to him. "Get the hell out of here, I'm watching the game."

The next day, Calvin called me to his office for an

explanation. He asked, "What's the deal with Hengen? He was all upset yesterday."

I responded, "Hengen wrote a very bad article about Boswell, and he was really upset about that. He told me that he was going to knock Hengen's lights out. Now, Boswell was lit up after only three innings and Hengen started following him. I knew that he was going to wait until he got to right field and punch him out when no one else was watching. Now do you think that I should have locked the gate? Or did you want to have Boswell suspended for punching a sports writer?"

That's all I heard about the incident from Calvin, he knew I did the right thing.

Calvin's employees were not always as loyal and trustworthy as he thought. Howard Fox called me into his office and took a ring out of his desk drawer. He said, "Calvin has been so good to me and my family, that we decided to get this ring for him to show our appreciation."

There was a big presentation in which Howard presented Calvin with the ring at a birthday party. After Calvin came out with his book, *Calvin-Baseball's Last Dinosaur*, he received a letter from Howard's wife, Yvonne. She wrote that she wanted the ring back since they didn't write favorable things about

Howard. Calvin had accused Howard of being out for his own good and a back stabber. Calvin told me, "I never wore or wanted the damn thing anyway." He then packaged it up and sent it back.

Showing professional sports on television and cable at frequent intervals was just starting to get big when Fox asked my opinion. Howard asked me what I thought about the early cable agreement for the Twins. I said, "You know, Howard, I don't like the deal. First, they want to show the Twins on TV and I don't think you should have to pay for something they want. I can't believe you would want to be a partner in their cable deal. Why would you want to be a partner, if they wanted to televise your games? If I were the owner, I guarantee that I would get them to pay me for television rights."

He said, " Ray, I feel the same way. Only, I hate that Clarkie. I would rather go on the side of Bruce and Billy."

Clark Griffith is Calvin's son and he advocated having the television companies pay to televise our product. Bruce Haynes and Billy Robertson wanted to put up a lot of money and be part owner in the cable company. The deal was a disaster and caused the Twins and Calvin to lose a ton of money. The lack of money also made it much more difficult for the Twins to sign talented free agents in the early eighties. Eventually, with the lack of large amounts of television/cable receipts entering the ball club's vaults, Calvin had to sell his team. Instead of acting in the best interest of the ball club, Howard preferred to go against his feelings and the correct decision because of a dislike of Calvin's son.

Movers were loading the semi-truck, after spring training was finished, to take equipment back to Minnesota. I looked at one point and they were just about finished loading the truck. When I looked back, they were taking the packed items off the truck again. I ran out to the movers. "What are you doing?"

"We have to unload this stuff. Howard Fox wants us to put his car in the truck. But don't worry, we'll ship this stuff a different way."

We had to send all our opening day bats by a different trucking service. This was an additional club expense, as well as worried the players who needed their bats. It turned out that the bats didn't arrive by opening day, all because Howard wanted to put his personal vehicle on the truck. The players had to use the small bag of bats we brought on road trips, rather than a better and larger selection of bats.

Howard used to go to Clancy's Drug Store often to pick

up skin cream for his wife, which was supposed to slow down the aging process. He would turn around and have the drug store bill the Minnesota Twins and entitled it, "Medication for the players." This was just another way Howard took advantage of his position in the organization. Howard's pettiness didn't stop there.

Every year, the ball players would sign dozens of autographed balls, which were given to various members of the organization. The Fox's sold dozens of these autographed balls at garage sales for fifty cents each. A blank ball cost the club much more than that, which is why I made Dave Boswell practice on the fuzzy fruit.

On the brighter side of the Fox story. Howard lost a ton of money by not holding onto the balls. Today, with the cost of memorabilia soaring, the balls would be worth a bare minimum of fifty dollars a piece. A signed baseball with just Carew or Killebrew is worth thirty to fifty dollars each.

Howard Fox is amongst the most two-faced individuals that it has been my displeasure to meet.

When Jimmy and Billy Robertson were with the ball club, Howard would always call them "brothers." Not simply because of their biological connection to one another, but rather he included himself as though they were all family. When they would walk by his office he would shout after them, "Hey brothers. How's everything going?" After they passed he would say to me, "Those guys couldn't get a job with any other club. Nobody would hire them." Still, in front of them he acted like their best friends.

Howard didn't like Tony Oliva at all. Every year, players are afforded the opportunity to buy some tickets to the post season games. Tony used to go around to different players and ask if he could buy their tickets from them. During the season, we would pass around a list of possible World Series and playoffs spots. Oliva would write down, "Oliva 12 (Oliva, Allison, Killebrew, Grant, Versalles, Battey)."

This upset Howard. If there had been any left over tickets, he could have taken them and sold them to his friends. Thus, Fox became upset at Tony for doing the same thing he wanted to do.

Houston Jimenez suffered because of Fox's ability to hold a grudge during his short stint with Minnesota. Whenever Fox was rubbed the wrong way, he found some way to get back at the person. If a player was a borderline baseball player, Fox usually nudged the negative way. I gave Houston the number one when he came to the Twins in 1983. Howard was very upset at this since that was the number formally held by the late

Billy Martin. Many people credit Fox with the ouster of Martin after winning the American League in 1969. I didn't want an executive telling me which numbers to give players. Seeing Houston in that particular number may have caused Fox to bring up old memories of his nemesis Martin. Perhaps it was my fault for giving Jimenez the number, but he only lasted in Minnesota one season.

Another player who irritated Fox was Ron "R.D." Davis. He was the player's representative and Twins' closer from 1982 to 1986. We had a player named Jim Eisenreich, who was diagnosed with Tourette's Syndrome. He was a Minnesota native and a really nice guy, but this disorder made him have an uncontrollable tic. He was sidelined for much of his time with the Twins, and had to be in the hospital. While he was incapacitated, Ron went to Howard and said that Jim was entitled to meal money. Howard disagreed with him, but looked it up and found out Eisenreich should receive the money. Ever since then, he held a grudge against R.D. Fox even approached me once and said, "You know what 'R.D.' stands for? Real Dumb. And I like the player representatives to be real dumb." Despite what Fox thought about Davis' intelligence, the club had to pay for Eisenreich's meal money.

* * *

David Koch was the president of the New Era Cap Company, which is one of the largest producers of professional baseball hats in the world. I placed a very large order with Koch, but Fox demanded that I cancel it. One of his cronies, Duke Zilber, had lost his job and found new employment with AJ Hat company in Richmond, Virginia. Fox wanted me to cancel the whole order so his friend would get the business.

New Era had treated us very well throughout the years, with good products and service. I went to Calvin's office and told him what had happened. Calvin said, "Ray, don't worry about it. You're the equipment manager and Howard's the traveling secretary. You place the order with whomever you want. I'll tell Howard the same thing I just told you." I don't know what Calvin said to Fox, but I didn't have a problem with the order after our meeting.

When Billy Martin started managing the Twins in 1969, we held a meeting. Billy wanted to set up rules on how he ran the team. His most important rule involved who would be in the clubhouse. He said, "I do not want any Tom, Dick, or Harry to walk in the clubhouse. If they do not work for the club, and they are not media, I don't want them in the clubhouse. If they do work for the club, let's say they come from public relations.

I don't want them to bullshit with the players. They are to say what they came to say and get out. As far as I'm concerned, I don't want anyone in the dressing room that isn't on the payroll, except Mr. Crump." The "Mr. Crump" that Billy referred to was my father who liked to be around the ballpark.

During the season, Wiesner told me that Billy wanted to see me and was very upset. He said, "That Foley Hooper doesn't belong in the clubhouse. I want you to get him out."

Hooper was Fox's golfing buddy. Howard was in the training room getting his ears cleaned and Hooper was waiting for him in the locker room. I said, "Mr. Hooper, I'm going to have to ask you to step outside. There's a rule that you have to be employed by the club to be in the locker room." Howard stepped outside and quickly came back in with a red face.

"You have just thrown out my best friend in the whole world." Howard was hurt and angry, but didn't have any right to bring guests into the clubhouse.

I looked at him and said, "Let me tell you something, I don't want to ever catch anybody in here who isn't on the payroll. You know the rules." He left, but it was another in a series of exchanges that we had.

Fox was a very devious individual. He tried to pick up

dirt on individuals quite frequently.

I remember I came into the locker room and he was searching Ken Landreaux's locker. I asked, "What are you doing?"

He continued searching. "I'm looking for drugs. He has to have some kind of dope in here."

When Howard searched Landreaux's locker he found nothing but dirty socks and jock straps. Yet, he was convinced that Ken must have known he was coming to search and removed narcotics.

This was typical of Howard's actions. He asked me to do things for him ranging from snooping through lockers and bags to taping players' union meetings. All of which was against the agreement between Major League Baseball and the Players' Association.

The 1965 World Series featured the Minnesota Twins versus the Los Angeles Dodgers. We won the first two games at home, lost the three on the road, and then won the sixth at home, but lost in the seventh game 2-0. At least I still have a World Series ring to further cement my fond memories of the occasion.

I wanted to take my new bride, Carol, to Los Angeles

for the World Series. I asked Howard, the traveling secretary, if she could come along. Fox said bluntly, "Calvin says she can't come."

When we were on the plane, I was sitting up front when Calvin walked by and said, "Raymond why didn't you bring Carol along?"

I didn't tell him why, because I thought it was pointless. Killebrew and Lemon both got on my case about my lack of disclosure.

The next time that we had a chance to go to the World Series in 1969, I told Fox that Carol was making the trip to the World Series regardless of whether she was on the team plane. He said, "Sure, sure, of course, no problem. Bring her along." I always said after that, if the team ever made it to the championships again, Carol would get the ring. Unfortunately, I never had a chance to fulfill my promise. (I was no longer with the club in 1987).

Years after this, when Carl Pohlad owned the club, Calvin asked, "Why didn't you tell me about that son-of-a-bitch phony Fox? I would have fired him on the spot."

"Mr. Griffith, you know you wouldn't have fired him. You believed in him so much, he was such a friend of yours."

Since then, I've heard that Calvin told Sam Mele, Bill

Rigney, and Gene Mauch the same thing he said to me.

Chapter 8

The Entertainers

Throughout my life, I have always had a fascination with meeting celebrities. The first major personality I met, discounting ballplayers, was Arthur Godfrey. He performed many benefits for the Red Cross. He came to old Griffith Stadium for a game and rode a horse onto the field, and jumped over some jumps. While he was there, I asked him about going to the Arthur Godfrey show in New York at Radio City Music Hall. I said "I know tickets to your show are sold out. I wanted to know if there was anything you could do to get me tickets since I'm going to New York City in a couple weeks and would love to see your show."

He gave me a private number to his dressing room backstage at Radio City, and told me to give him a call when I got into town.

I went on this road trip with the Senators when I was fifteen. The trip took me to Philadelphia, New York, and Boston by train. It was one of my greatest thrills. In fact, it was probably the first time I had ever spent several nights away from home. We arrived at the New Yorker Hotel very late since the train was delayed, and I only had about ten minutes to get to the auditorium before they closed the door for the show. So, I picked up the phone and called Arthur Godfrey and he told me to come right over. I was a very excited young kid, not even old enough to drive. I jumped into a cab in front of the hotel and ordered, "Take me to Radio City."

The driver crossed the street and stopped. With a sly look on his face, he said, "Here you are. That'll be $1.50."

I wasted some money I had saved for the trip by taking the taxi across the street, but I made the show with Godfrey's tickets and was treated great.

My favorite memory of Metropolitan Stadium in Bloomington, Minnesota, involved the Statler Brothers. They had come to a Twins game on August 31 and Tom Mee, the Twins' public relations director, asked them if they would sing the national anthem. They politely refused, instead they opted just to enjoy the ball game. I got a call from Frank Quilici, who told me to come out to the field right away. Normally, the only time I was called into the dugout during a game was when a player was injured. If a serious injury occurred, the trainer and I would carry the player back into the training room on a stretcher. So, I ran down the runway toward the field, and I expected to find a dilapidated player.

A close friend of mine, Mel Schroepfer, had told the Statler Brothers that it was my birthday. The Statler Brothers were singing "Happy Birthday" to me from the press box upstairs during the seventh inning stretch. It was much more thrilling than my twenty-eighth birthday, in which I was thrown into the shower by the players while completed dressed. The song was the most cherished moment of my life at Metropolitan Stadium.

The Beatles came to the Met for a concert in August, 1965 and stayed in the locker room. They needed to stay away from hotels that were constantly besieged by groupies who constantly surrounded their rooms. I had pictures taken with each member and the entire group. In addition, I had a baseball signed by all four. The ball is probably the only one in existence. It is extremely rare, valuable, and amongst my most prized possessions. It used to be displayed in my Minneapolis baseball museum, but was deemed too valuable to remain in that location.

They arrived at the stadium at one and their part of the show started eight hours later. They had come from the charter terminal at the airport, where their private plane was parked far away from the terminal to avoid a large crowd formation. They immediately hopped into a limousine and came to the stadium. I was asked by their promoter to take care of the clubhouse while the band was there.

The four men from England were mesmerized by all the lockers and equipment. They looked around like children in a candy store. They were especially impressed by the locker of Harmon Killebrew, who was famous even overseas. In addition, they discovered a sauna for the first time and a couple of them even used it during their visit. Throughout their visit, the Fab Four were polite and well-mannered.

The band held a press conference in "The Minnesota Room" at the old stadium. As they were leaving for the meeting, Ringo Starr said, "Ray, I want you at our press conference."

I still have no idea why this was important to him, but I followed his request and accompanied them to the media event of the year. John Lennon placed his arm on my shoulders as we walked by many state troopers on the way to the room.

The Beatles all acted very odd at the press conference. It was a complete turnaround from the way they presented themselves earlier in the clubhouse. Not necessarily different from the way the public perceived them, but rather different from when they were alone.

Their actions reminded me of professional wrestlers acting different on and off camera. At the press conference, the four swung their arms around and acted crazy. When, the door was closed to the locker room, they were much more conservative. They acted more like businessmen, instead of crazy rock n' roll stars. They were very professional, and knew unequivocally how to promote themselves.

Brian Epstein, the Beatles road manager, needed to get someone to sell the souvenir programs for the concert. He asked me to find some honest people to sell the programs for the band. Of course, the first people I thought of was my bat boys. This allowed them to earn some extra cash, and meet the most popular band in the world.

After the bat boys sold the programs, they returned with the money and gave it to the road manager. The proceeds from the sales were immediately split equally by the five of them. They brought in a roulette wheel and sat on the floor and gambled until one person possessed all the money. I have a picture of this occurrence in the museum. Brian and the Beatles must have done this at each venue, since they were so nonchalant about its occurrence. Paul was known to have more money then the other band members. Presumably, he was luckier than the rest at the wheel.

I had my picture taken with the entire band together. I was also fortunate enough to be photographed with George, Paul, Ringo and John individually. When I had a picture taken with one of them, another would take the picture. Then, we rotated. I understand now that I am one of the few people that have pictures with the entire band. Another was Ed Sullivan. I've heard that Sullivan had a clause written into the entertainers' contracts that stated they must have a photo taken with him.

The Beatles' limousine was parked in front of the clubhouse door. People had surrounded the car because they knew the guys would have to go to it when the last song was over. Meanwhile, the state troopers had a difficult time containing the crowd. The mob screamed and swayed back and forth around the vehicle. When the concert was over, the band jumped into a parked, linen truck, sat on fold-up chairs, and headed toward The Leamington Motor Inn in Minneapolis without many people noticing.

I walked outside the clubhouse, and quite a few people were still standing around the band's unused getaway car. A girl recognized me and asked, "Weren't you the guy that was with John Lennon?"

Like an idiot, I answered, "Yes, I was."

She ripped the sleeve off the shirt I was wearing and ran away.

The Beatles had an underaged girl at the Leamington, and the police could have prosecuted them. Don Dwyer, the current Chief of Police for the City of Minneapolis, decided to let them go. The girl was there of her own free will, and it would have cost the city too much money to return the Beatles to the city for a trial.

After the excitement died down, I was contacted by an advertising agency that was working with Dayton Hudson department stores. They gave me eight hundred dollars for the sheets and pillow cases the Beatles had laid on while waiting for the concert. This was still in 1965 and the eight hundred dollars amounted to a very good day for me. The sheets were then cut into small portions and a drawing was held for them in the teen department of their stores.

Often times when I met celebrities I would give them a token of gratitude. I concocted a care package of Twins t-shirts, hats and autographed balls. I received a thank you card from the entertainer, George Hamilton IV, which I thought was quite amusing. It said, "Thank you for the balls, my kids are outside right now playing with them. He didn't know that they were valuable, and weren't meant for people to play with them.

For years, I have traveled to the entertainment capital of the world, Las Vegas. I have a close friend from Chattanooga, named Charlie Cox, who worked at the Frontier Hotel in the city. He would set up complimentary hotel rooms for us, and free meals. In addition, he could get us into almost any show we wanted to see while there. The only concert he couldn't get us tickets for was Frank Sinatra. Carol and I were walking down the strip when we saw the colossal billboard advertising Sinatra's appearance at Caesar's Palace. We stopped into the hotel, and while Carol used the rest room, I jotted down a quick note to Sinatra. The note read:

Dear Mr. Sinatra,

You don't know me, but we are big fans of yours. We tried to get reservations for your show, but were unable to do so. I would like to ask a big favor of you. We don't want complimentary tickets, we would like to get reservations for your show. We would gladly pay to see your performance. If there is anything you can do, please give me a call. I am staying at the Frontier Hotel in room #314.

Thank you very much, Ray Crump.

I handed the note to the clerk at the front desk and waited for my wife. Soon, Carol returned from the rest room and we left. I didn't tell her that I had left a message for Sinatra.

Bill Cosby is a good friend of mine. I met him when he was just starting out in the comedy clubs. We arranged to meet with him in a restaurant after I left the letter for Sinatra, because we wanted to take a picture with him for our Christmas card.

Every year, my wife and I produced a card for family and friends that chronicled the entertainers whom we had the fortune to meet in the previous year. After we had our lunch, Bill invited us to his opening show the next night and suggested that we come backstage after his concert. We agreed since we couldn't get tickets to Sinatra and went back to our hotel.

Once we got to our room, I went downstairs to the casino while Carol stayed in the room. We were going out to dinner that night with Joe Guercio, Elvis Presley's band leader, and his wife. This was after Elvis had passed away, and Joe was working at the Hilton Hotel. Anyhow, Carol stayed in the room, because she wanted to fix her hair for our dinner that evening.

While she was in the room, the phone rang. The voice said, "This is Frank Sinatra's office calling. Frank received your message and wants to know how many are in your party."

Carol was confused by the voice, since she didn't know I was trying to get tickets.

"There are just two of us."

"Okay," said the voice. "Just go to the VIP line at the hotel tomorrow and there will be two tickets waiting for you."

Carol thanked the kind voice and I returned to the room. She said, "What's the deal with the Frank Sinatra tickets?"

"I left him a note when we went to Caesar's Palace."

"Don't you remember that we are supposed to go to Bill Cosby's show tomorrow?" Carol wasn't as excited as I was about getting the Sinatra tickets. I never dreamed that we would have to choose between the two entertainers.

But after all, I saw it as a challenge when Charlie Cox, a man with numerous connections, couldn't get tickets. Frank Sinatra's show was always sold out due to the fact that Ceasar's Palace made it a point to cater to their guests by offering them tickets first. It was rare for people to turn down the opportunity to see one of the most famous men in the country. It was quite funny when Charlie found out we had tickets, he simply shook his head in disbelief.

I still had to answer Carol's question.

"Yes. But, I thought it would be kind of nice to see Frank Sinatra's show, since we never have been to it before."

Carol gave me a nasty look, but didn't say a word.

The next night, we went out to dinner that night, as planned. While we were eating I asked for Joe Guercio's advice on the problem of having two show dates for the same night. He said "Frank Sinatra had been talking of retiring lately. I don't know if he will or not, but if you have never seen his show then you should go to it."

"What about Cosby?" I asked. "He is leaving us tickets, and we are supposed to meet with him after the show."

"I wouldn't worry about that. Bill will probably have a couple of drinks and not even notice that you're not there."

Carol was very reluctant to go to the Sinatra show. She said, "Our first invitation was to the Bill Cosby show. So, I think we should go there. In fact, I'll go to the Cosby show and you can go by yourself to see Frank Sinatra."

I finally got my way and we went to the Sinatra show. Before we left for the concert, I made plans to go meet with Roy Clark after his show. He was playing in the Frontier Hotel. My brother Donald, who was also in Las Vegas, wanted to meet him. I had met Roy Clark on one of several trips to the Grand Ole Opry in Tennessee. With all this under control, we left for the Sinatra show.

I suggested to Carol that we leave the show early, before

the encore, to meet my sibling. She was very disturbed by that. We had seats right next to the stage, and she thought that Frank Sinatra would notice the empty seats. I agreed with her and we planned on leaving immediately after the concert was finished.

What I didn't know was Sinatra and Cosby had gone to a fight together before their concerts. Sinatra invited Cosby to come over to the hotel after both of their shows. Cosby declined because he was meeting with us after the show. They did some detective work and discovered that they were talking about the same "Ray Crump from Minnesota." They decided to have a bet, in which they would page me immediately after their concerts. If Sinatra's page was answered, Cosby would lose and vice versa.

My page came right on time after the Sinatra show. When I answered the white courtesy phone, I was asked if I had paid for the show. I started to think that it was the maitre d' cops wanting payment for the meal. I also was somewhat annoyed since I was late in meeting Donald. The person on the line said "Mr. Sinatra would like to take care of your bill." We waited near our table and the waiter returned with our money.

We finally made it backstage at the Roy Clark show, and everything worked out well. The next day, we had an early flight back to Minneapolis. I decided to drop over a couple of

Minnesota Twins autographed balls to Frank Sinatra. I wanted to show my gratitude for the tickets to the show, and for the payment of our bill.

When we arrived back in Minnesota, I took a part-time job during the winter at LaBelles' department store. I didn't want everybody at the ballpark to know that I had this job, but I told the receptionist where I could be reached in case of an emergency. Judy Walk, the Twins' receptionist, was contacted by Frank Sinatra's office. She told Frank Sinatra's secretary that I wasn't available. They went back and forth like this for several days.

Finally, Sinatra picked up the phone after his secretary had reached the Twins' offices. He decided to show his secretary how to get the job done, by using name recognition.

He said, "Is Ray Crump there?"

Judy answered exactly as I had asked. "No, he's not."

Sinatra asked, "Is he going to be there tomorrow?"

Again she replied, "No, he's not."

He was getting a little irritated now. "Is Ray Crump out of town?"

"No, he's not. He isn't out of town."

"Well, could you please give me a number to reach him?"

Once more she answered as instructed. "I am not at

liberty to give you that number."

Frank thought his name might do him some good. "Well, this is Frank Sinatra . . ."

"Yes," she replied. "And this is Lily Tomlin."

A few days later I was at home watching the news when Carol answered the phone. She called me to the phone and I was surprised to hear Frank Sinatra's voice. He told me the story about the Twins' receptionist. He also said, "I'm good friends with Tommy Lasorda, and I really appreciate the autographed balls. I understand it's thirty degrees below zero there. I want to take you and Carol out to dinner the next time you're in Las Vegas, Los Angeles, Hollywood or any place warm."

Months later, we received a letter from him saying that he wanted us to come to Vegas as his guest for his new show. When we arrived, he was holding a reception for Joe Lewis before opening his five day show at Caesar's Palace. Rod Carew had just won one of his batting titles and was at the show. We went up to the VIP window again, and we sat by the stage as we did on the previous occasion.

Marilyn Carew shouted at us from high in the "rafters" where her and Rod were sitting. They asked if they could sit with us. I wanted very much for them to sit with us, but I didn't feel it was our place since Frank placed us at the table. Howard Cosell was seated in a booth next to our table, and he invited Rod and Marilyn to sit with him. My dilemma was solved.

After the show ended, Carol and I immediately left. I wasn't aware that Frank Sinatra had wanted us to go backstage after his concert. His office called our hotel several times, but we had gone to see Bobby Vinton's show and returned very late. The next day, my wife and I went to see Glen Campbell perform. I was walking through the Desert Inn hotel and heard, "Paging Ray Crump. Paging Ray Crump. Ray Crump, please pick up the courtesy phone."

I picked up the courtesy phone and Dorothy Uhlemann, Sinatra's secretary for over seventeen years was on the line. She said, "Frank has been trying to reach you."

"That's funny," I said. "We've been gone all day, and we are leaving for Minnesota tomorrow morning."

"Frank wants to meet you. He's on stage right now, and would like to meet you after he gets off stage. Can you come over here now?"

I, of course, agreed to meet with the entertainer. She asked, "What are you wearing?"

I informed her I was wearing a blue suit.

"Okay," she said. "Frank's personal body guard will

meet you at the front desk, and he's wearing a dark brown suit."

We went back to the hotel. Calvin had said that he and Charlie Dressen had met Sinatra a long time ago in Washington. Calvin asked me to get an autographed ball from the singer if I ever met him. I went to the front desk and met the large dark suited man. He took us on a strange path to meet Sinatra. We went back down small hallways, through the kitchen, and finally to the dressing room. There was a guard standing in front of the room who asked, "Are you Mr. and Mrs. Crump?"

We responded affirmatively.

"Mr. Sinatra gave me instructions to let you into the dressing room. He will be with you shortly."

We went into the dressing room, and we could hear his music through a PA system in the room. Frank walked off stage singing into his cordless microphone. He carried the microphone and sang down the hallway until he stopped at the door of his dressing room.

He handed the microphone to the guard at the door. "I don't want to be disturbed by anyone. I have good friends with me."

When he turned to us, he said, "I want to thank you for the baseballs." He continued, "I'm sorry we didn't get a chance to meet sooner."

"Oh, the balls were nothing. I would like to get a picture with you to put on our Christmas card."

"Absolutely," said Frank as Carol pulled the small easy-to-use-one-step camera from her evening bag. Frank said, "Wait a minute" and picked up the phone. "This is Frank Sinatra. I want a cameraman sent down to my room. Thank you."

Sinatra started to rearrange the furniture throughout his room. He didn't want any of his furniture to be in the photograph. He even moved his big jar of Tootsie Rolls, his favorite candy, out of the frame. We lined up for the picture. He was in the middle, and Carol and I were on his left and right sides respectively.

Frank said, "Wait a minute. The lady is always the center of the picture. No lady should be on the end in a picture." He realigned us to place Carol in the middle of the shot. We felt that the star should be in the center.

The camera man did his job, and I asked Frank to sign the baseball for Calvin. He signed the ball and verified that they had previously met. He signed Calvin's baseball, "To Cal, best wishes, Frank Sinatra."

In addition, he signed one for me. "To Ray, best wishes, Francis Sinatra." His secretary, Dorothy, said this was one of the only items she has ever seen in which he used the name, "Francis." She said, he used that name exclusively for business documents. The sad aspect of this story involved Calvin's memento. He loaned it to the Twins to display for a short time. Someone broke in and stole his baseball out of a display case. I understand that the ball was ruined by the thief playing catch.

When we left the dressing room, "Kojak," Telly Savalas, was waiting to meet with Frank. We snapped a picture with him for the Christmas card. When I was leaving, the bodyguard walked us back upstairs. He smiled, "You know what? That Telly Savalas is an ass."

"Why is that?" I asked him.

"When he tried to get into to see Frank, the guard wouldn't let him. So, he figured you must be a friend of Frank's and he felt he had better pose in a picture with you."

I thought that was funny as the devil. After I got back to Minnesota, I sent Frank and his wife, Barbara, some Twins t-shirts and shorts. A few months later, I received a call from Bill Cosby. He said, "Ray, I don't care how much it costs, I want you to send me something."

"What's that?"

"I want you to send me a real Twins hat and some shorts. The other day, I played tennis with Frank and Barbara

Sinatra. And they came onto the court with t-shirts, shorts and golf hats with Twins on it. I want shorts and a real Twins hat. I'm playing tennis with them next week and I want to walk out on the court wearing nothing but Twins paraphernalia."

I sent out the package Federal Express the next day. Since then, Frank Sinatra came to Minnesota a couple of times during the summer months. I needed twenty tickets for his sold out concert on one occasion. I offered to pay for all of them, but he gave me four free tickets for my family. He is a very kind and giving person.

In 1968, I was in the clubhouse when the phone rang. On the line was a young Hank Williams Jr., who didn't know me from Adam. He was over at the Hilton Hotel in St. Paul and wanted to come see the ball park. I said, "There's not a lot to see here right now, but you're welcome to come over."

He hopped in a cab and came right over. He was nineteen years old at the time, and appearing at the Minnesota State Fair. I showed him the clubhouse, the field, and I took him to the offices to meet Calvin.

Calvin said, "Why do you wear cowboy boots, they are so damned hard to get on and off?"

Hank didn't respond verbally. Instead, he smiled and

kicked his foot in the air. His boot went flying through the office with ease. Calvin was so impressed that he gave him some World Series pins and other valuable mementos.

I took the young singer over to a distributing warehouse for Wilson Sporting Goods. He picked up a few gloves and catcher's gear and then we went to introduce him to my family.

When we got to the house, there was a note on the door that said my son had an accident and was at the hospital. Andy , had run into the corner of a wall in our apartment. Andy had been kept inside for nearly a week, since my youngest son had just been born. When he was finally allowed outside, he crashed into a wall and needed several stitches. When we got to the hospital, Carol and Andy had already left. W e went back to the house, but the trip to the hospital made Hank late for a press conference. I drove him back to the hotel, and his manager was very upset. Hank told me, "I don't care about a press conference, your son is more important then a press conference." He is a great guy and nuts about baseball.

Hank's whole entourage would play baseball when they went to different cities to play. For example, if they came into Minneapolis, they would call the local fire department and try and arrange a game. Once he came to town with a different drummer. I asked, "Hank, what happened to the drummer?"

"I had to get rid of him."

"What?" I asked, "I thought he was pretty good."

He continued with a serious look on his face. "He was a great drummer, but I had to get rid of him. He couldn't catch. We were losing ball games because of him. I had to get another drummer that could catch."

Tony Orlando came to the Carlton Dinner Theatre which was next to Metropolitan Stadium. I had met him years earlier while vacationing in Las Vegas. It was 1981, and the Twins had just played their last game ever in the ball park. He called me at home and said he wanted to show me something and he sounded very excited. Tony Orlando and his manager had jumped the fence surrounding the Met to go jogging in the parking lot. Tony had found an old program from the last game played at the stadium. He showed me the book and said, "This is going to be worth a lot of money some day."

Another person whom we saw at the Carlton was Mac Davis. He loved playing in Minnesota. He said he could have earned a lot more elsewhere, but he loved the area. When he came to Minnesota, he would drive out to a golf course and ask to join someone's foursome. He said this was the only place he could go where no one would bother him with autographs or photographs. His son came over and I took him through the clubhouse and he worked out with the team. When Mac found out his son was working out with the club, he jumped up and came over from the hotel. With camera in hand, Mac took dozens of pictures of his son during the workout like a proud father.

When Larry Gatlin came to the Carlton, I arranged for him to work out with the team. I got him a uniform and he was ecstatic. He put his arms in the air and said, "You know Ray, this is like heaven. It's a great feeling to work out with a professional baseball team." His eyes were glowing and he had a smile from ear to ear. In fact, we have a picture of him in a "Gatlin" uniform made especially for him.

George Jones and Tammy Wynette were performing a concert together at the Carlton. They had been married at one time. Tammy was already in Bloomington, and George's bus was heading toward the Twin Cities. While George was riding to Bloomington, a TV movie about Tammy Wynette was playing in the bus. In the movie, they had the actor that portrayed George hitting Tammy.

George got very upset at this version of their marriage and when the bus stopped at a truck stop, George hitched a ride back to Tennessee.

The owners of the Carlton were upset about this unscheduled trip. If George Jones didn't appear at their club, they would have to refund the ticket receipts. In addition, much of the money was already spent on advertising and related expenses. Eventually, George calmed down somewhat and came to Minnesota.

I received a call from George and his manager, who said they wanted to come to a game. I took them to the game and seated them in Calvin's box near the dugout. When the radio announcer, former Twins' infielder and manager Frank Quilici, saw me he didn't know who I was bringing to the box. Yet, he knew that I often brought entertainers to games. He announced over the radio that he assumed it was a country music star, and would find out which one.

Karen Olson, the owner of the Carlton with her husband, Ken, had an employee overhear the announcement on WCCO and she immediately called me. She asked me to sit with George and make sure he didn't leave until they talked. I did as she asked, and George performed that night. Karen was so happy that she had a headliner, she gave me complimentary tickets to the show. George had also given me tickets, which I gave to Dick Martin (the trainer), Rick Stelmaszek (coach), and Tommy Wescott (bat boy).

I gave the ticket to Wescott on the agreement he would shout when Tammy walked on stage, "Hey George, hit her one more time."

I thought people would think it was really funny, because of all of the publicity that the press gave the movie.

I was sitting on the first table next to the stage, and the other guys were behind us. She walked on stage and I didn't hear anything. I was kind of perturbed at this, but found out that Stelmaszek and Martin threatened to slap him if he shouted anything. When I think of it, I was relieved Tom listened to Martin and Stelmaszek.

One of Ray Jr.'s favorite ballplayers was Danny Thompson, who played for the Twins from 1970-1976 and died that year of leukemia. My son was at home and received a call from the entertainer, Danny Thomas. He said, "Is Ray there?"

My son said, "No, may I take a message?"

"This is Danny Thomas and . . ."

Ray Jr. interrupted him and said irritably, "That's no joke, Danny Thompson died!"

My son angrily slammed the phone down. He thought someone was joking around with him, and it upset him very much.

I finally received the messages and tried several times to get a hold of Thomas. In fact, I called on three separate occasions, and each time I was told I would be called back. Eventually, I contacted him and he said that he was hung up on so I explained the story. That night I went to Danny Thomas' concert, which incidentally was attended by the Vice-President's wife, Muriel Humphrey.

Danny took a little note from his pocket and read it on stage. He got on his knees and rose his right hand into the air and said, "I swear on my mother's grave this is true. The message read, 'Danny, yoohoo called and you are supposed to call him.' Yoohoo was supposed to be Ray."

The message meant that Danny was supposed to know immediately who had called, but he was clueless. It's just a story that I'll never forget.

I met the late Roy Acuff at the winter baseball meetings in Orlando, Florida. Bill Anderson, the country and western star, had a group of entertainers together to perform at the convention. While Bill and his band were on stage, I noticed

Roy Acuff was sitting alone at a large table so I joined him. I introduced myself and we became very good friends. When I would go down to spring training, I would drive through Nashville and I would go to the Grand Ole Opry. I called to get tickets one year, but they were sold out. I picked up the phone and got in touch with Roy. He said, "Don't worry about it, Ray. You'll have tickets waiting for you at the door. I also want you to come back stage and see me."

When I arrived for the show the tickets were waiting for me, just as promised. I was sitting in the audience for the show as Roy was performing. When he was done with his act, Wilma Lee Cooper appeared on the stage for her set. As she began her act, Acuff ran back on stage. He had his jacket and tie off, he grabbed the microphone, and said, "I just want to say something. I forgot, I have a real good friend here. Ray Crump and his family, I want them to come up here by the stage so we can go backstage."

Wilma Lee, who had been in our house before, said, "Roy, he's not only your friend. Ray is a very dear friend of mine, also."

Carol and I love Wilma Lee. She is such a sincere lady and we wish we had the opportunity to visit with her more often.

* * *

The Christmas cards that my wife and I produced each year became quite the anticipated commodity during the holiday season. Every year, the cards would document the changes in the lives of my family and detail forty or fifty entertainers we had met during the year. After I met someone, I would put them on our mailing list and send them a card.

Don Rickles arrived in Minnesota for a concert at the Carlton Dinner Theatre. He asked the owner if I was coming to the show, she checked the computer and discovered that I was attending the concert. When he was in the middle of his act, he stopped and asked for someone to turn on the house lights. After they facilitated his request he said, "I'm looking for a friend. Ray Crump, I want your ass backstage after the show."

When I went backstage, he took our Christmas card out of his brown leather bag. He pointed to the different pictures on the card. "Here you've got Kenny Rogers, Jerry Lewis, Dolly Parton, Wayne Newton, and you don't have my picture. Where's my picture?" He made a big scene out of this and ripped up the card and threw it all over his dressing room.

He grabbed a camera out of his bag, and handed it to his manager. He said, "Take a picture of Carol, Ray and me. And I better god damn well be on his Christmas card next year."

The next year he made the cut and was on the card.

I knew Roy Clark from about 1953 in Washington D.C. When I first met him, he never sang a word. He played backup guitar with Buck Owens in Jimmy Dean's band at bars. For a short time, he even had Patsy Cline in the band. I went to see him at "The Famous," which was a bar in a very rough neighborhood in Washington near the bus depot.

Later, I planned on seeing him at a new club called "The Starlite." There was a greater-than-usual amount of hype about the opening of this new club. It had been in the works for several months and there was much anticipation about the opening night. Right before Jimmy Dean's band was supposed to play there, Jimmy fired Roy Clark.

After his dismissal, Roy started to drink a lot. At nine o'clock at the new club, Jimmy Dean walked on stage. I heard a loud crash through the swinging doors at the back of the club. Roy had driven his motorcycle through the front doors and roared toward the stage. The police immediately arrested him and took his driver's license away.

A few years later, I was watching "The Merv Griffith Show" and the audience asked him about the incident. He freely admitted what he had done. He also added that Jimmy Dean had every right to fire him, and he would have done the same thing.

Roy Clark was over at our house in Bloomington after the club had moved to Minnesota. He said he was only going to stay twenty minutes, but stayed much longer. His manager kept looking at his watch, since Roy had an eight o'clock show. Eventually, he told Roy that they had to leave for the concert.

Roy does not like anyone to tell him what to do and ignored his manager's request and stayed for a few hours. In fact, he became more adamant about staying. Eventually the manager asked me to see if I could get Roy to leave. I talked him into leaving and he made the show in a nick of time.

Roy likes to keep himself occupied until seconds before his appearance on stage. This, undoubtably, drove his manager nuts. Entertainers have different ways of preparing themselves for an opening and I firmly believe that this is Roy's way of coping.

I liked to go to a bar in Minneapolis called, "The Flame." I told Ray Perkins, one of the owners, that he should get Roy Clark to perform at his club. Perkins agreed and Roy came back to town. He borrowed someone's car [After he got his license back] to go to a Twins game at Metropolitan Stadium. When it was time to leave, Roy discovered his car was blocked by another. In all the years I was around the stadium, I had never heard of this happening.

Roy called the bar and said he was going to be late. When he finally made it to the bar, Perkins said, "This is going to cost you thirty-three dollars."

They had some kind of agreement that performers had to arrive early for sound checks or rehearsals. Roy made five hundred dollars a week for performing there and was now being docked. Roy packed the place every night he went on stage. I went to one of his concerts that week when Roy received a telegram stating that one of his songs was being released, "Fingertips."

When this stint was over, Perkins paid Roy and asked him to come back in six months.

Roy said, "It'll cost you a lot more next time."

"Well, how much more?"

"Thirty-three hundred," Roy responded seriously.

This was a huge jump, obviously, from five hundred. Roy was still mad about being docked thirty-three dollars.

Perkins was shocked at the jump. "Thirty-three hundred? Where did you get that amount?"

"Well," Roy said. "You were going to dock me thirty-three dollars, so I want thirty-three hundred dollars."

"Roy, I'm not going to dock you."

"I don't care, I want thirty three hundred dollars."

Perkins wouldn't hire him, but that would have been dirt cheap. Two months later, Roy started "Hee-Haw." The biggest country music show ever on television. Several years ago, Roy experienced chest pains. His doctor said, "If you live through this, you will have to change your lifestyle."

Roy laughed at the doctor's bedside manner. He was scared to death and bothered at the doctor's blatant statement. Some people need to be gently persuaded to slow down, but this harsh advice didn't help Roy feel better.

The Grand Ole Opry in Nashville is a haven for country music fans everywhere. Some performers went on tour to the Carlton Celebrity Room in Bloomington. I went backstage and I talked to Bill Anderson, who was singing and in charge of the group. While there, someone came up to Bill and said they had to be out of their hotel room at 3:00 p.m. They were concerned about what to do in the period between the concert at eight and the time they had to leave the hotel room.

I overheard the conversation and said, "Bill, I have a small house in Bloomington, not too far from here. I wouldn't mind if the group wanted to come over to my house. We could have a little cookout. Between my Rec. room, living room, and patio, we should have enough room for everyone."

He agreed to come over with Jeanne Shepherd, Wilma Lee Cooper, Melvin Sloan, The Tennessee Travelers, Jimmy C. Newman. In addition, these performers brought their bands with them. Fifty or more people and six buses rolled down my quiet street for the barbecue and I led the way.

I knew there were many people involved, but I wasn't aware that everyone had their own bus. Our street doesn't have much parking available for the forty-foot tour buses, but they could stretch themselves up and down both sides the street.

My neighbor, Hel Morvig, came over to look at the busses and try to figure out why they were there. He is the type of person that everyone has in their neighborhood. In other words, he always has to know what is going on with everyone. He asked me about the buses and I responded with a straight face, "I'm having a party tonight. The band just came and is starting to set up."

He looked at me so strange. Meanwhile all the neighbors, who didn't often venture outside their homes, had decided to investigate. We never saw so many people coincidentally out for a walk. We all had a good time and the group still remind me of the barbecue whenever I see them.

After all, they are often on the road and they spend too much of their time in hotels. Sometimes they would prefer to be in someone's home for dinner.

Freddie Fender, a country singer, played a concert at the Carlton. He told my wife and me to come see him backstage after the show. After the show, we told the security guard our names and Freddie was expecting us. He said, "Freddie is too busy to see anyone right now. You'll have to leave."

We didn't think it was a big deal, so we left. It's not really an uncommon occurrence. Sometimes, an entertainer will tell you to come back stage and the person at the door doesn't know or doesn't care. The next night, Freddie called us and asked what happened to us. I told him the story and he invited us over to his hotel. When we arrived, he said, "I want you to come to my show tonight."

"We've already seen the show." I tried to explain to him.

"No," he continued. "I want you to come back so you can point that security guy out so I can punch him right in the mouth."

Freddie Fender is the type of person whose threats should be taken seriously. The limousine arrived to take him to the show. The driver jumped out of the car and it happened to be the security person from the night before who wouldn't let us go back stage.

When he saw us, he immediately recognized us as the people he had turned away the previous night and tried to make amends. When we arrived at the Carlton, the security guy said, "Can I get you anything? Something to drink? Anything at all?"

He had overheard Freddie talking about punching him in the nose, and was trying to avoid the possibility. He even put chairs on the side of the stage for us to sit. In fact, as Freddie sang, he directed his words toward Carol.

My sister-in-law, Pat [Burton's wife] was staying at our house in Bloomington. I had a surprise for her, I was going to take her over to meet Bob Hope. I didn't tell her of my plans and I was still at the ballpark when the phone rang. My wife was taking a bath, so Pat answered the phone.

Bob Hope said, "Is Ray there? This is Bob Hope."

"Yea," Pat said. "Come again."

"No, seriously this is Bob Hope."

She's kind of a nervous person, but she finally recognized his voice. She assumed I was playing another one of my practical jokes on her, but I was innocent.

"Carol, Carol, you have to come out here." She

shouted.

I had him sign a program for Pat's mother who absolutely adored Bob Hope, but I had inadvertently left it at his hotel room. He called to say that he was afraid to leave it at the front desk, because he thought someone would take the program. I was supposed to call him when I arrived at the hotel, to get the program in person. I was amazed at how concerned he was about us receiving the autographed book.

Carol and I went to Dolly Parton's concert at our favorite locale, the Carlton. Carol made a cake in the shape of a guitar for Dolly before her show, and I dropped it off at her hotel. While she was on stage, the singer asked someone to turn on the house lights.

"Is Ray Crump here?" She asked trying to peer into the crowd and blinding lights.

I remained quiet.

"If anyone is sitting next to Ray Crump, will you please get him to stand up?"

Still I didn't move since I didn't want to call too much attention to myself.

"Well, Ray gave me a cake before the show and I think he doesn't want to stand up because his wife doesn't know about it. Anyway, I want to see him after my show."

When she finished her concert, Carol and I started to head backstage when we were accosted by some friends and acquaintances who wanted to go backstage with us. I didn't feel it was right to bring along everyone I knew, so I politely refused all of them. One of our neighbors even asked us to get her to sign a family bible.

My wife and I arrived backstage to meet with Dolly between her two shows at the Carlton. We talked for awhile and her manager came by to tell her to get ready for the next show.

"Three minutes, Dolly." He said before walking away.

She acknowledged him and continued talking.

"Two minutes."

Again, she kept talking to us.

"One minute."

Dolly turned to us and said, "They won't start the show without me. They better not dare and start the show without me."

As we continued to talk, her music was overheard in the background. She jumped up. "You know what? They have started the show without me."

And she ran out of the dressing room and onto the stage.

* * *

One of my all-time favorite entertainers is Ferlin Husky. I met him in 1957 at the Fairfax County Fair in Virginia. When I first met him, he was one of the top country performers in the country.

Over the years, I have found Ferlin always enjoyed life to the fullest. He has always wore white suits from the early days until today. Ferlin married a fellow singer named Marvis, who was from Minnesota. Together they performed at the Flame Cafe in Minneapolis.

Ferlin had triple bypass surgery in Miller Hospital in St. Paul. Since Marvis was staying at the hotel during his long recovery, we asked her to stay with us in Bloomington and she was delighted. Ferlin was also allowed to check out of the hospital and stay with us in between his check ups.

Meanwhile both entertainers frequented the Twins' games at Metropolitan Stadium. While he was in the hospital, he played jokes on the entire hospital staff. He'd listen to Twins games and throw out his Twins hat in the hallway for someone to retrieve. If they were losing, he'd lie on the floor with the door open so someone would think that he had fallen or collapsed.

Elvis Presley was in Ferlin's band when he first started out in the entertainment business. In fact, according to Ferlin, he taught Elvis how to water ski during the early years.

While Ferlin was in the hospital, Elvis' father, Vernon, called the hospital to check up on him. I happened to take the call from Mr. Presley, and assured him that Ferlin would pull through.

Calvin Griffith is also a great fan of both Ferlin and Elvis. The three of these people seem worlds apart, but admired each other for their contributions.

We recently visited with Ferlin and his daughter, Jennifer, in the new Branson, Missouri, entertainment complex. He went out of his way to show us a wonderful time. Ferlin set up shows for us, invited us to lunch and to his home. It truly was one of our most enjoyable vacations, except for the heat and traffic. We do owe a debt of gratitude to Ferlin and Jennifer Husky.

In 1972, Jackie Kahane called me in the clubhouse of Metropolitan Stadium. Jackie was the comedian who opened for Elvis before his concerts. Jackie was trying to obtain an autographed photograph of Rod Carew for his nephew.

We were playing a day game and I invited him over to the game and met him at the press box. In the Twins locker room, I introduced Jackie to Rod Carew and he signed the picture. To make matters more exciting, Rod also gave him a bat. To reciprocate, Jackie offered us tickets to the Elvis concert.

I thought this was hilarious. When the tickets went on sale, Jim Wiesner and Mickey Guiliani [who ran the souvenir department at the Met] went down early in the morning to try and get good seats. I thought seven in the morning was too early to wait in line, so I slept while they waited in a long line. When they received their tickets, they talked non-stop about the upcoming concert. They made it clear that I didn't have tickets. They were right about the fact that I didn't have tickets. At least until Elvis' comedian came to visit.

As we walked down the stairs of the Met Center for the concert, I ran into Mickey Guiliani and his wife. They were dismayed upon seeing me.

"I thought you weren't coming to the concert." Mickey was shocked to see me.

"Well," I said. "I just got these tickets today, so I figured I might as well go see the show."

I left them in the forty-ninth row and continued to walk to my seats in the fifth row on the main floor. I watched them track me further and further down the stairs. The closer I came to the stage, the more irritated they became. Mickey said later that his wife was complaining to him on every step. She reiterated, "You should have let Ray get you tickets."

Jackie had opened up for Wayne Newton in Las Vegas before landing a spot in Elvis' caravan. Elvis liked Jackie's performance and told Colonel Tom Parker to make sure he became the new opening act.

At first, Jackie was reluctant to join Elvis' troupe, since he had been working with Wayne Newton for a long time. Eventually, he acquiesced.

Wayne had only allowed Jackie five minutes to warm up the crowd. It usually takes a comedian more time to get into the groove of his act. The Colonel promised him he could take was as long as he liked. This was all he needed to hear and he took the job.

Jackie warmed up Elvis' frenzied crowds for seven years, until the rock n' roll legend passed away. Jackie gave the eulogy at the King's funeral and came out with a tribute that captured his feelings for the entertainer, which we play in a section of our museum.

Elvis' wanted to play at Metropolitan Stadium. When I use the word "play," I am not talking about singing. He wanted to play a pick up baseball game against the grounds crew at the Old Met. I talked to Calvin Griffith about the possibility, in fact,

Calvin reminded me of the story, and he was excited about the prospect. The plan had been to lock the gates to keep the media away. Unfortunately, Elvis died before his wish could reach fulfillment.

Elvis' road manager was Joe Esposito. Elvis was enthralled with his manager and trusted him. If Joe told him to stand on a table, he would do so without question. This is contrasted to the Colonel, whom Elvis respected but didn't always follow his instructions.

The Colonel was a grand manipulator, who often used Elvis as a puppet. Occasionally, the Colonel would pull Elvis' strings too hard or the wrong way, and Elvis would explode. On the other hand, Joe Esposito was very concerned about the King's health and well being. He would never do anything with regard to furthering Presley's career if it would hurt him in any way.

After Elvis died, Joe Esposito became the road manager for the Bee Gees during the height of their stardom following the release of their soundtrack in the *Saturday Night Fever* film.

We also became close friends with Joe Guercio, Elvis' band leader. In fact, whenever Elvis and friends came to town, Guercio and Jackie Kahane came over to our house after concerts. Once again, the neighbors peered out their windows and were curious about us cooking steaks at four a.m.

It seemed that the two or three times I was with Elvis, I never had a camera available to take a picture with him. Every time I met him, it was a last minute opportunity. The one time I remembered the camera, I was too embarrassed to ask for a photograph since many people were around.

Charley Hallman, a writer for the *St. Paul Pioneer Press*, was covering Elvis' trip into the Twin Cities. I had never heard of the guy before he wrote an article about Presley. I think he covered hockey or some other sport that I didn't pay much attention to.

Charley had seen me at Elvis' concert and in leaving his hotel room. He approached me in the clubhouse and asked what I thought of the show.

"I have seen him perform better." I responded.

I felt bad about saying that, but I didn't know he was writing a story on Elvis at the time. I thought he was simply a guy asking a question. The next day an article was in the paper, which I have displayed in our museum, criticizing Elvis' concert.

I sent the article to Jackie Kahane and Elvis and explained that I had felt bad about what had transpired. Jackie told me that "Elvis said, 'That's one of the better articles written about me. Don't worry about it.'"

Elvis' took an interesting journey on one of his trips to Minneapolis. He was known for some of his eccentric behavior. Late at night, following one of his concerts, he drove to see "Mary Tyler Moore's" house. He was quite excited about seeing the house, so I assume he liked her show.

Every time I go into a nursing home, I get sad when I see the patients incapacitated with drugs. My mother, during her last few years, was like that. The people in the convalescent homes, that I've seen, try to make lives easier on themselves by subduing the residents.

I asked Elvis to sign some pictures I had taken of him in concert. Elvis was strung out on drugs and signed some pictures twice, or started to sign them twice and didn't realize what he was doing.

The distant looks of some nursing home residents is the same thing that happened to Elvis Presley. He was continuously fed pills in between concerts. It was easier for his handlers to give him pills than to risk him doing something wrong in public. The Colonel didn't care about Elvis, he only cared about money.

Elvis liked to go out into the public. He wanted to go bowling and other simple things, like the time when he wanted to play baseball at the Met. But, the people around him thought this would be a bad idea and they wanted to control him.

They would give them pills until he was about to perform a concert. Soon they would gradually get him off the pills for the concert and after it was over, more pills were administered. It became so bad that Joe Esposito told him he would leave if Elvis' didn't check into a hospital. Esposito had been gone for several months, and Elvis finally checked himself into a hospital. Joe returned shortly before his death.

I had talked to Elvis about appearing on our Christmas card, but he was reluctant. It was April, 1977, and Elvis was concerned about his growing obesity. Thus, he declined to have his photo taken with Carol. He promised to let us have our photo taken in Las Vegas when he performed there in December. He must have believed that he had the ability to lose the excess weight by that time. Elvis died on August 16th, my youngest son's birthday, and we never did get our picture taken together.

Calvin Griffith didn't recognize country music singer, Bill Anderson while on a plane to Minneapolis.

Carol and I stand among members of the hot country group Alabama.

Dolly Parton visited the Carlton Celebrity Room in Bloomington and we met backstage for a picture.

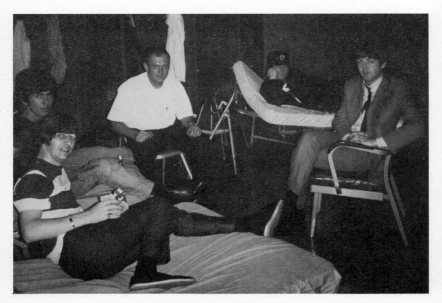

The Beatles came to Minnesota for a concert in 1965 and stayed in the locker room before the show.

**I came to Minnesota with my former boss, Calvin Griffith,
one of the great contributors to baseball.**

**Telly Savalas posed for a picture with us, since we were
important enough to pose with Frank Sinatra.**

**The flamboyant Liberace was as proud of his
rings as he was of his piano playing.**

**The Statler Brothers sang "Happy Birthday" to me during
the seventh inning stretch at Metropolitan Stadium.**

Bob Hope was so concerned we wouldn't get an errant program he handed it to us personally.

Wayne Newton was just one of the entertainers we've seen in the entertainment capital of the world

**The late Hubert H. Humphrey, the former
Vice-President, was a good friend of mine.**

**Bill Cosby was pitted against Frank Sinatra
one night in Las Vegas. Bill lost.**

**Jerry Lewis in one of the most amusing
entertainers I've ever met.**

**Mac Davis is getting a little too cozy with my
wife in this photograph.**

Roy Acuff recently passed away, but I will always remember meeting him at the winter baseball meetings and in Nashville.

George Jones was my guest at a baseball game when he was supposed to be preparing to go on stage.

Tony Orlando is sure he stumbled upon a valuable program as he jogged by the Met.

**Frank Sinatra made sure Carol was in the center
of our picture taken backstage at Ceasar's Palace.**

Carol and I found George Burns to be a very kind man and a fabulous entertainer.

Kenny Rogers is a favorite entertainer of ours, we've met him on many occasions.

Danny Thomas once called my home and accidentally upset my youngest son.

Don Rickles was amazed that he wasn't on our Christmas card one year and took steps to correct the problem.

**Larry Gatlin is a huge sports fan. Once, I arranged
for him to work out with the team.**

**Ferlin Husky is one of our best friends in
the entertainment industry.**

**I've known Roy Clark from the very beginningof his career.
Here, he poses with my sons, Andy and Ray Jr.**

**One of Freddie Fender's underlings was fearful that Freddie
would take revenge because he failed to let me backstage.**

**Although I met Elvis on several occasions, I never seemed
to have a camera ready to capture the moment.**

Chapter 9

My Life and Endeavors

I tried to get into the Army Reserve without success. They were not taking any new recruits. The program consisted of six months active duty and then five and half years of reserve duty. I thought this way I could continue working during the baseball season and could finish my military duty during the off season. This was a much better alternative for me then spending two years straight with the regular Army.

In the Summer of 1958, I received a letter from the draft board requiring me to report to Fairfax, Virginia for military duty. I went out to Griffith Stadium and told them that I needed to report. A ticket manager, Johnny Morrissey, had a lot of clout with different Congressmen and military officials. He said, "Ray, I understand you have been called up for military service."

"Yes, I have."

"Do you want to go?"

"No," I answered.

"What if I could get you in the Army reserve? Would you want to do that?"

"I would like that very much."

"Let me see what I can do for you."

One of his friends at the Pentagon was General George C. Marshall, a five-star general. The General had just retired, but kept an office at the military headquarters. Morrissey called his friend and told him my problem. I met with General Marshall the next day at his office. Colonel George, the General's aide, offered me a cup of coffee. I declined saying that I preferred hot chocolate. I didn't realize the significance of being a general in the United States Army. The general told me he would try to help and sent me home.

A week later, Colonel George called and told me to go to the Reserves Center in Arlington, Virginia. This was the same center that I had been visiting, but they lacked openings. By that time, the government had closed the center down to new recruits. I sat in the building and waited to be called. An officer walked past and said sternly, "How can I get it through your head, we're not taking any new recruits."

"I'm waiting for Lieutenant Myers." I responded in a polite and militaristic way.

"I'm Lieutenant Myers. Come into my office."

I followed his order and entered his office. He looked very serious. "Let me ask you a question. Is your father a Congressman?"

"No, sir."

"Is your father a Senator?"

"No, he isn't"

"Is he a top government official?"

Again, "No."

"What does your father do for a living?"

"He's a steam fitter." I answered earnestly. "He puts in air conditioning and heat."

He said, "You take this test. And when you're finished, you come see me."

I went into the other room. When I finished the test, I returned to his office.

"When do you think you'll go into active duty?" The Lieutenant still had a stoic look on his face.

"October 7th." Colonel George and I had already chosen that date, since it coincided with the end of the Senators' baseball season.

"No way." He answered, "We have waiting lists of six months to a year. There is no way you can get in that soon. It's impossible."

When I went back to the stadium, I was very concerned. I didn't want to miss any of the upcoming baseball season. I called Colonel George, and told him what had happened. He said, "Don't worry, the wheels are turning."

I only went to one meeting during my six years in the reserves. The program stated that reserve soldiers were supposed to go to the meetings once a week, but it often interfered with my baseball schedule. I just couldn't make it to the meetings.

In the meeting I did attend, I was called for active duty.

Lieutenant Myers seemed surprised. "What date is he going in on? October 7th?"

"Yes, October 7th." Answered the man with the clipboard.

"And what transportation is he taking?"

"Air," replied the lower officer.

Normally, Army reserve members traveled by train or bus.

The Lieutenant was still very interested in my orders. "Where is he going? Fort Bragg, North Carolina?"

"No sir. He's going to Fort Knox, Kentucky."

The Lieutenant was mystified by this assignment. Not only was I allowed into the Reserves, but I also served on the date I chose and I went there by air.

When I arrived at Fort Knox, all the enlisted men and draftees were separated. I was in a section with twelve other men. Included in this group were: future Twin Mudcat Grant, and Phil Linz who was eventually an infielder for the New York Yankees.

While I was in basic training, my grandmother died. The Army had a rule that explicitly stated that a soldier would be allowed to attend funeral services of a deceased relative only if they lived together. My grandmother did not live with me, but I called Colonel George who arranged for me to be excused.

When I returned from the funeral, I was called to the Orderly Room. General Marshall had called my mother and asked for my address. Captain McBride, who was in charge of my battalion, was waiting for me. He looked nervous. "Private Crump, are you unhappy here at Fort Knox?"

"No, sir."

"Is something troubling you?"

"No, sir."

"Did you write to General Marshall?"

"No, I didn't sir."

"Why would General Marshall write to you, Private?"

"He's a friend of mine, sir." I responded with a smile this time.

He handed me the letter from the General, which asked if everything was going well, and dismissed me. It was difficult for him to believe that I would be corresponding with such a highly decorated General.

Later, I received a phone call from John Hillerich of Louisville Slugger Bat Company. He invited me to visit his company to watch the bat-making process. I had to decline since no one was permitted to leave basic training for sightseeing. He was very insistent and inquired, "Would you like to come if you could get away?"

"Sure," I responded.

A couple of days later, I was in formation in front of the barracks. A Sargent approached me. "Private Crump," he said. "You get a Class A uniform on. A car is coming for you to take you to Louisville Slugger."

A long black limousine arrived and I asked another serviceman to tell the driver to drive three blocks ahead. I didn't want Grant, Linz and the others to see me getting into this car while they still had to work. I arrived at the bat company and was treated extremely well.

After basic training, we had to cross the stage to receive our diplomas from Captain McBride. He handed me my hard earned certificate with the comment, "Put in the good word for me at the Pentagon." I didn't return to Fort Knox until the Senators played in an exhibition game against the Reds.

* * *

While I was the visiting clubhouse man in Washington, I used to work at a furniture store when the Senators were out of town. I needed to work at Brothers Furniture Store to supplement my income while the team was on the road.

Whitey Ford, the Yankees pitcher, called me to place bets on horses for him. He had a friend at the Charleston Race Track in West Virginia, who worked with thoroughbreds. I made a call to a bookie for Whitey and placed his bet. Meanwhile, the guy I called placed his own bet with another bookie, since he knew Whitey was very accurate with his picks.

Whitey called me on five different occasions. There were two other men who worked in the department with me. It turned out that every time Whitey called, one man wasn't at the store. Thus, my colleague and I placed bets on Whitey's pick. The first four times, the horse came in first and we made a killing.

The man that kept missing out on this opportunity, said, "I don't care what happens. If Whitey Ford calls again, I want you to place one hundred dollars on the nose for that horse."

When the fifth call came from the future Hall of Fame pitcher, we all jumped at the possibility of making an additional "sure thing" bet. The jockey, in this race, was Yanzee Kratz. I called after the race to see how we had done. The man that answered the phone said, "The horse won the race, but the jockey fell off the horse at the finish line."

I hung up the phone and started laughing. Upon telling my co-workers that we lost due to the jockey falling, they said, "You shouldn't be laughing, you should be crying."

I thought it was funny that the one time the guy placed his bet, he lost a Franklin quickly.

In 1963, I had an apartment in Minneapolis on twenty-second and Nicollet. This was before Dave Boswell became my roommate. When I went over to the apartment building, the caretaker said that she didn't want to rent to me since I was single. She was afraid that I would tear up this brand new apartment complex with wild bachelor parties.

I said, "Let me tell you something. I don't drink much, and I don't have parties. I work at the ball park and leave early in the morning and return late at night. I travel half the season with the team."

She still seemed concerned that I was going to throw parties. I said, "Look, I'll make you a deal. If I throw any parties, you can ask me to leave and I will immediately." Finally, she agreed to let me stay.

I was on the first road trip of the year, when I received a delivery at my apartment. At the time, the Twins had Hamm's Beer Company sponsoring the team. This company sent a case of beer to the players, manager, the coaches, and the equipment manager. They delivered the beer directly to our homes. A couple of other breweries in the area, Schlitz and Grain Belt also sent cases of beer to us. By coincidence, Ted Culbertson, a good friend of mine, who owned a liquor store in Hopkins, also sent me a case of liquor. Since I wasn't home, these deliveries were made to the caretaker's apartment. When I got back into town, I went to the apartment and found a note to go the caretaker's apartment. It was about two in the morning, so I decided to wait until the next morning.

When the sun first appeared, I walked downstairs and knocked on her door. The caretaker opened it with a disgusted look on her face. She said, "For someone who doesn't drink and doesn't have parties, you have a lot of liquor here."

I reassured her that I hadn't ordered the liquor and that it had been given to me. She still had a hard time believing that anyone would give away booze free.

My best friend, as I was growing up in Virginia, was Andy Payne. He and I were so close that our personal experiences often mimicked one another. In fact, I named my first born after him. As we grew up and I entered the baseball world, we started to grow apart. Still, I kept my winter home in Annandale, Virginia, and we spent much of the off-season together.

Andy's step-father became very ill and needed twenty-four hour care. They had run out of insurance and we all took times sitting with him. I would stay with his father, Barkley, all night. I had to leave my shift when it was time to go to Minnesota to pack for spring training, but I left my family in Virginia.

I drove to Minnesota and packed the equipment and I was heading to Florida for the pre-season, by way of Virginia. When I returned to Annandale, I decided to stop by the hospital to check on Barkley.

The nurse said, "Mr. Hodgson has expired."

This was the first time I had ever heard that phrase associated with the death of a human being. I always heard it connected to a parking meter. I left the hospital and told my dad what had happened.

My father used to always go to the track, for as long as I can remember on Saturdays, but he said he would go to the funeral parlor after the races. When he came back from the track, he packed his car for Florida, since he was going to follow me down South the next day.

While he was packing, he suffered a massive coronary and he was rushed to the hospital. My mother called me and I immediately drove to the hospital. My dad was quickly brought into the emergency room.

The doctor said, "Mister Crump, what did you do today?"

"I went to the race track."

"Well, how did you do?"

"Not too good. I ended up with thirty-two cents." My father was sitting up though they had wanted him to lie down.

"Mr. Crump, please lie down."

My dad said, "I can't lie down. I have to go to the mortuary to see Mister Hodgson. He just died."

I was standing in the same room as my father when the doctor made a statement that frightened me.

"Mister Crump," he said. "If you don't lie down, you'll be in the mortuary. Just lie down and relax."

He sounded terribly serious. I think this is the first time I actually knew my father was close to death. He died Sunday evening.

At the funeral home, someone asked Andy why I wasn't

there and someone else said I was at the hospital.

Andy went over to the hospital, and the doctor told him that my father had "expired." Andy's step-father died Saturday and my father died Sunday. Barkley was buried Monday, while my father was buried Wednesday. Throughout our lives and the deaths of people near us, Andy and I have always been close.

I took my mother, Violet, to Red Wing Pottery in Minnesota. As we were driving there, I was pulled over by a state trooper. My mother was all upset as the trooper asked for my license. He said, "Are you the Ray Crump with the Minnesota Twins."

I responded affirmatively.

"I figured so. I was clocking your car speeding. When George Mitterwald (the catcher) dropped the ball and let in that run in . . . You sped up an extra ten miles per hour."

He didn't give me a ticket, but warned me others would. Thus, being a member of a baseball organization was very advantageous at times.

I've never been very involved with politics in my life, which makes this story interesting. A woman was running for the city council and stopped by my house to campaign. I don't even remember her name now, but she said she was going to stop by five thousand houses. She said that even if the people weren't home, she would keep coming back to their house. I was impressed by her effort and ardor. I promised to help her if she went to all five thousand homes. I received a call from the woman wanting me to fulfill the promise. I took campaign material to five hundred residences for this woman. When I got to the polling place, I looked on the ballot and shouted to Carol, "Oh my God, she's a Republican!" I had never voted for one before and her literature didn't mention it, so I assumed she was an independent. I just remember everyone in the polling place telling me to "pipe down."

Earl Battey was beaned in the head by a fastball in Boston. I didn't make the road trip, but I saw the incident on TV. Doc Lentz, the Twins trainer, called me and said we should do something to protect the players against these injuries.

So I went to Snyder's drugstore in Bloomington, and picked up some foam materials. Next I went a few stores down to a Hardware Hank, and picked up some sheet metal, rivets, and a can of paint. After that I went back to Metropolitan Stadium and I made a side piece to go on the helmet. I went up to the maintenance shop and Dick Ericson, who was in charge of the stadium, helped me rivet the side piece and the foam onto a helmet. Finally, we spray painted it blue to match the rest of the helmet.

When the team came back in town, I put the helmet in Battey's locker and went to have dinner. While I was eating, Battey saw the helmet and took it to the field with him. When he was on the field, a member of the Associated Press, asked Doc Lentz to pose with Battey and the new helmet. The next day that photo went nationwide. The caption made it appear that Lentz invented the ear flap. At the time, Ericson and I didn't think anything of it, we just thought it was funny.

After the season, I called Mr. Lindsey Wolf at the American Baseball Cap Company. I asked him if he could mold this side piece on the helmet for me over the winter, and I sent him the helmet. He agreed, and that is how side pieces were first molded on the side of helmets. Now it's almost impossible to find a helmet without an ear flap. I should have patented the device.

Later I received a call from Lindsey who said that they were having a problem with Wilson Sporting Goods. It turned out that Wilson was copying the ear flap design, which the American Baseball Cap Company had patented. He asked if I could sit and meet with their patent attorney, because they were going to subpoena me to court about the original design. Wilson Sporting Goods contended that the ABC Co. didn't have the right to patent the piece since Doc Lentz made it. Apparently he had been going everywhere and telling people that he invented the piece. It's just so funny that he got all the recognition for making the helmet for Battey and another one for Ron Santo, the Cubs third baseman. Dick Ericson and I just laughed at it, when we could have made ourselves rich.

Tony Oliva endorsed a product called "Tony O' Super Grip." Oliva used to always throw his bat into the stands. In fact, once he even hit a lady. A man from Roseville, MN, named Bob Haasl who owned a company called Plasti-Dip International, called me. He said he thought we could come up with something to solve Oliva's bat throwing problem. He said that since I knew people in baseball and he knew a chemist at his company, he thought we could work together and market this product. The super grip was a can of a sticky substance to be applied to baseball bat. It's purpose was to eliminate the use of the "pine-tar" rags.

We made this product for Oliva, and then Howard Fox gave some cans to Arnold Palmer to take to the Pebble Beach Golf Classic. He was having a lousy day, but was still reluctant to put any substances on his clubs. Yet, it started to rain and there was nothing to lose, so he put some on his clubs. He also gave a can to Jack Nicholas, who won the entire tournament. A few days later I received a call from Palmer, who wanted to get fifty cases of this adhesive chemical. After conferring with Haasl, we decided to try and market "Arnold Palmer Super Grip." Palmer told us to contact his agents in Ohio. They informed us that we needed $50,000 up front to do any endorsements at all with them. I told them to forget it, but Palmer decided to do the project with us free. We put this wonderful item in the Labelle's stores in Minnesota, but we didn't have the backing that we needed to make it a large success.

In 1977 I had the idea to change the regular navy "TC" hat to red. Since we owned the rights to the concessions at the stadium, I thought this would be a good way in increase revenue. So we used the navy hats for all our road games and a new red "TC" hat for the home games. In addition, we came out with red shoes for the players to wear at home. I believe the year after that the Cincinnati Reds started wearing red shoes as well.

I also helped design professional baseball team luggage

with Pedro's Luggage of St. Paul, Minnesota. A few teams bought these bags such as the New York Yankees, but until this time nobody really had official team luggage. Later, I also helped develop equipment bags for the team. Calvin Griffith liked the Twins team to be dressed in suits and ties. He also didn't want them to bring along carry-on valets. He always wanted his team to look professional when they traveled.

Another product I was asked to help promote was called "Power Swing." The "Power Swing" had wings that looked like the inside a washing machine and players would attach their bat to it. The idea was to swing the bat, and the "wings" would provide wind resistance. The resulting pressure would help your swing become more powerful. I tried to get some players to use this item, but they were extremely reluctant. They were afraid of the odd shape of the device, and didn't want to look bad. I hopped on a plane and headed down to the All-Star game in Kansas City. I brought three one hundred dollar bills, and I saw Reggie Jackson warming up. I said "Reggie, all I want you to do is put this thing on your bat and take a couple of swings for $300."

He agreed to participate and walked onto the field. He took a couple of swings with our device attached to his bat. We received national exposure from this event, but it's something that could never happen today with the amount of money the players are making. Today, it would cost thousands and thousands of dollars.

Camilo Pascual and I decided to go into the hamburger business in 1962. We wanted to open up a McDonald's franchise, which would have cost us a total of $25,000 up front. We were discussing this when Sid Hartman, the sports' columnist for the Minneapolis *Star Tribune*, walked into the room. He said, "Listen, I know all about these drive-in hamburger restaurants. I had one on Hiawatha Avenue in Minneapolis. Don't waste your money. This McDonalds thing will never make it." We took his advice and every time I see a McDonalds, I think of Sid.

Incidentally, I learned the reason Sid was so knowledgeable on hamburger drive-ins was because he had the first Dairy Queen in the State of Minnesota (located near Minnehaha Falls). All I can say is, "Sid, you blew it." Stick with sports and real estate, you'll do better.

In the fall of 1981, from beneath the grandstands at Metropolitan Stadium I could hear a loud roar of people chanting, "Calvin! Calvin! Calvin!" Calvin Griffith, the man who brought professional baseball to a farm in Bloomington, had gone to the Twins Room after the game. A police officer had to get him onto the field. The police wanted Calvin to go down to the field in an attempt to quell the crowd, because it was feared that they would rip up the stadium." The Vikings had yet to complete their season, and people were already beginning to take pieces of history. This is one of my fondest memories of the old stadium, thunderous applause for an important contributor to the national pastime.

The following season, the Met Stadium was dismissed favoring the Hubert Horatio Humphrey Metrodome. Before they built the stadium, we all gathered around to determine how much space each department would need. The Minnesota Twins had to pay for their offices, kitchen, dining room, and the Twins locker room. The Metropolitan Sports Commission paid to build the Gophers and Visiting clubhouse, while the Vikings paid for their locker room. Thus, the state lacked rights to either the Twins nor Vikings locker rooms as long as they play sports in the Metrodome.

Calvin asked me to draw a diagram of my requirements for the new stadium with regard to lockers and storage spaces. At the Old Met, I used five separate equipment rooms to store various items. For the new facility, I wanted to build one large room to take place of the previous five storage spaces. I measured all five rooms, and used those statistics to determine the size of the Metrodome's equipment room.

I went to the meeting with my diagram of the new equipment room. The architects went around to everyone at the table and asked them how many feet they desired or required. The club was obviously trying to keep space at a minimum since they had to pay by the square foot. When they got to me, I told them I needed X amount of space for the locker room and X square feet for the storage area. Clark Griffith and Bruce Haynes threw their arms up in the air, became of the space I requested. They had looked at the original blue prints for Metropolitan Stadium. The plans showed one small room for the equipment, but I actually used five rooms. The small room had been put in place for the Minneapolis Millers, not the Twins.

Clark and Bruce walked back and forth in the Conference Room of the Met and said, "Do you realize how much space you're asking for?"

I retaliated. "You don't know what you're talking about. You've never worked a locker room. I have five equipment rooms here, not just one. I gave those figures by adding up all five rooms."

They reiterated, "You don't need that much."

Calvin stood up and looked toward the architects. "Take down those measurements, and build the equipment room to his specifications." The architects built the new equipment room as directed.

Calvin asked me to go to another meeting in St. Paul before they built the stadium. The architects were showing the plans to different people who were moving into the Dome. The plans had our locker room positioned in centerfield, while the Vikings lockers were to be located on the third base side of the field. We played eighty-one games a year in the ball park, and they only played ten. In addition, they didn't even use the dugouts, since football players stand on the sidelines. Upon my suggestion, they switched around the locker rooms.

The other suggestion I made at the meeting called for a separate tunnel for the umpires. The original plans would have had the umpires use the same runway as the home players. This never would have worked. Players can get very upset during a ball game and this was an accident waiting to happen. When I left the meeting, I was thanked for helping make a more user-friendly stadium. But, I merely pointed out the obvious.

Everything was not well with the new stadium. There were more problems than the highly publicized ones like air conditioning. When they made a small kitchen and a big dining room. They neglected to make space for walk-in coolers, kitchen storage, walk-in freezers and refrigerators. It almost appeared as though they had been building for a residence, rather than a large business dining room. Finally, they had to take over the equipment room for which I argued so strongly. I was forced to use a room in centerfield. If I hadn't made such passionate arguments for the large equipment room, the stadium would have had much bigger difficulties.

Don Poss, who was with the sports commission at the Metrodome, asked me to try to get the players to wear rubber spiked turf shoes like they do in football. Even if I could have talked our players into wearing turf shoes suitable for the new Metrodome carpet, I would have a difficult time convincing the superstars of baseball to wear the new shoes. Apparently the cleats were ripping up the turf. I said, "You know if that's what the commission wants, they should have built one stadium for football and another for baseball if that's what they wanted." He followed this request by asking me to get the players to stop chewing tobacco. It's clear that the sports commission really didn't know what they were talking about with regard to stadium design, construction, or player make-up.

An interesting turn of events happened in regard to the

Dome's teflon-coated roof. Heaters were installed that would melt the snow on top of the roof during the winter. Apparently, this was not a cost-effective mode of snow removal. Instead, maintenance personnel from the stadium would climb up the stairs to the roof with metal shovels in hand.

This was not a good idea. The shovels weakened the roof to the point where it collapsed. The stadium commission convinced the roof company to replace the damaged section without charge even though it was caused by a feeble attempt to save money.

During the 1991 World Series, Shirley Evans was sitting outside our store crying. I asked her what was wrong and she responded that she had been trying for weeks to get a ticket to the game. I felt sorry for her, and fortunately, I had an extra ticket to sell her for the game. She stopped crying and looked as though she thought I was an angel. After the game was over, she returned with her ticket stub in case I wanted to put in our museum.

The part of this story that I didn't know, my wife told me a short time later. The woman told her that she had been sitting outside Metropolitan Stadium in the rain waiting for a ticket for the 1965 World Series game. She had been told that the tickets were sold out, but they might find some for people that waited. Eventually, she was told that their were absolutely no more tickets available. Then, I came upstairs and saw her, learned of the problem, and returned with a ticket for her. I had forgotten all about this story since it happened decades ago, but it was a wonderful coincidence and Shirley visits us regularly.

**Rod Carew poses with my children in the days
he was a Minnesota Twin.**

**Harmon Killebrew holds my children for
a quick photo at Father-Son day at the Met.**

**My mentor, Fred Baxter, and I as we looked
during my days in Washington D.C.**

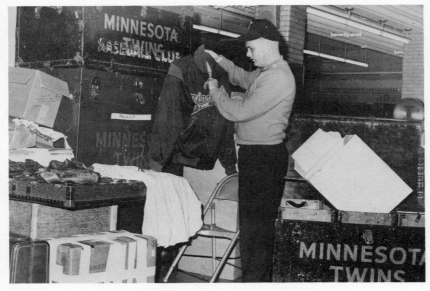

**Unpacking large trucks of equipment was
one of my many jobs as equipment manager.**

**Dean Chance is one of the many ballplayers who
has visited me and signed autographs at my museum.**

My parents, Welford and Violet Crump, enjoyed a quiet time in Virginia during the early 1950s.

**A clean shaven Hank Williams Jr. held my son, Andy,
when he was only a few years old.**

My 1965 wedding reception was nearly interrupted by the Twins winning the American League.

The whole family enjoying an outing at Met Stadium.

Here, I am adding a bottle of Vitalis to an All-Star's locker in order to supplement my income.

I'm preparing for another trip to Florida for spring training. It was hard work, but at least it was warm down South.

**Tony Oliva, my son Andy (Center), and
Scott Haasl advertise Tony O' Super Grip.**

Camilo Pascual and me during the olden days at the Met. He could have made a difference as a scout for Minnesota.

Chapter 10

The Business

When I left the Minnesota Twins on May 28, 1984, I decided to go into business for myself. I decided to re-enter the screen printing business and started RC Promotion Company with my wife, Carol. My oldest son, Andy also worked with us. My youngest, Ray Jr., was a sophomore in high school and completely uninterested in screen printing. Besides, he still worked for the Twins and Vikings selling souvenirs. We opened the new business in Bloomington on July 16th of the same year.

I had been in the screen printing business for seventeen years while I was still with the Twins. We printed t-shirts, jackets and other items. Many items were imprinted with Twins logos and sold in the stadium. In 1986, Mickey Giuliani, who ran the novelty department, came to our business in Bloomington and ordered $7,000 worth of shirts. Once the order was finished, I was told by Mickey that the Twins had decided to get the shirts overseas where they were less expensive.

I was very upset about having all this money invested in the t-shirts with no place to sell them. I drove down to the Twins offices and tried to get them to follow through on the agreement, but they declined. When I met with them, they asked for my purchase order. In the seventeen years I had done business with the club, they had never asked for a purchase order. A precursor to a new era under Mr. Carl Pohlad.

As I walked back to my car, I saw a "For Lease" sign on an old yellow building across from Metrodome. Upon calling the number attached, I discovered that the hundred-year-old building was being leased by Control Data Corporation. Don Crowe was in charge of the building at the time, and I arranged to rent space from him.

The building was owned by Joe Bramson, and was used to produce furniture for a century. When the Dome was being built, a row of buildings stood across from the new Metrodome. Cowles Media Company, who own the *Star Tribune*, and the city combined to condemn the buildings. The lots were then razed to make parking lots. When they came to Bramson's building, he fought the condemnation. He spent days in court, but won after agreeing to make many internal changes. He had to install sprinklers, work on the elevator, and many other expensive updates to the building. Bramson had many battles with Cowles Media, but he won and was allowed to keep the building.

Between 1984-85, Dave Moore, who was a vice-president for the Twins, approached Bramson to rent the building. Moore wanted to use the new building for the accounting staff at the Dome. He agreed to lease the building if Bramson installed air conditioning. They wanted the building to be ready for the All-Star game in 1985. They were planning on throwing parties and then turning it over to the accountants. Bramson did what was asked, but the Twins reneged on the agreement.

Joe Bramson was extremely upset over this latest occurrence and vowed never to let Cowles Media Company or Carl Pohlad gain control over the building.

Despite my friends and business associates' advice, I rented the building from Control Data who had leased it from Bramson. My accountant, Richard Schachtman was against me entering the business, because he thought I would have a difficult time competing with the Twins. I have always felt that if you offer lower prices, people will come to buy your products. Schachtman didn't think the consumer would worry about the price since they would be willing to pay for the whole experience. He warned me that even if people did come into the store, the Twins were not going to welcome the competition.

I brought the concept of a small snack bar and souvenir store with me to Minnesota after obtaining it as a youth. On the first trip I made with the Senators as a teenager, we stopped in Boston. Right next to Fenway Park there was a store selling Red Sox souvenirs. The image never left my mind. Even the whole time I was with the Twins, I dreamed of opening a shop next to a major league baseball stadium. My sons had worked in the stadium selling souvenirs while I was still with the Twins, and learned the business through experience. With my family behind me, we accomplished the goal through much hardship.

Another friend, Max Levine didn't think I would do well in Minneapolis either. He suggested that I buy a large flashing neon sign saying "Public Restroom." He said that I would need a way to attract people to come into the store. I wasn't too thrilled with this concept in marketing. At least the owner was excited that I wanted the building for a store, rather than a parking lot. Bramson was delighted about my plans for a souvenir and snack bar, but offered a warning as well. He said, "Ray, go get them. They'll battle you, but just battle them back. You look like a fighter."

Bramson was a volunteer at the University of Minnesota's cancer ward and promised to donate the building to them on his death. He told them they could do whatever they wanted with the building, except sell it to Cowles Media Company or Carl Pohlad. Bramson was still upset at the treatment he received from both of the businesses. When he passed away in early 1987, I received a call stating the building was for sale. I was not in any position to buy. The previous six months, in which I occupied the building, I lost $68,000. My accountant advised me to get out of the business. I said, "What if I tell you that I'll make money next year."

He responded with sincerity. "It's impossible. You should just cut your losses. There is no way you can lose $68,000 and then come back and make a profit."

Since, I was financially unable to buy the building at the time, I continued to rent. All the money I had saved from my career in baseball had been put into the business. If I would have approached a bank for a loan to buy the building, they would have asked to see my financial statement. As soon as they saw the large loss and my lack of assets, I would have been laughed out of the office. The time to buy the building was not at hand. Still, I did have a two-year lease on the building with an option for four additional years.

Carol was very reluctant about the opening of the business, or shall I say cautious. The paramount concern for her was the $60,000 rent. I was convinced that the place had the potential to be a gold mine, despite my friends who were doubting the venture.

In 1987, the Minnesota Twins won the World Series for the first time. Before the first post season game began, I had printed up t-shirts that stated, "Where the West was Won." The newspaper printed a picture of the shirt and the Minnesota Twins took the newspaper clipping to Judge David Doty. (Judge Doty was the same official who had presided over the recent free agency in the National Football League.) The judge permitted the federal marshals to raid our establishment and confiscate the alleged counterfeit shirts. We had made $2,700 on the day the marshals, reporters and Twins officials came in the store. All this amounted in free publicity.

The next day we took in $35,000, followed by $27,000, and the final day we took in $29,000 and ran out of Championship merchandise. Everyone was crazy for Twins merchandise and people were standing in lines stretching down the street to get into our store. My son, Ray Jr. was attending the University during that year, and walked around the corner. He saw the huge line and tried to sneak his way in the store. People started to get upset since they thought he was just another customer. He said, "Hey, let me give you some advice. If you let me in, you'll get your merchandise faster because I work here." The line opened like the Red Sea and he walked through.

Since the World Championship, we have drawn on a

large base of people and hearsay to thrive in the business. School kids, senior citizens, and various other groups and individuals have visited our stores. We have had 10,000 people go through the store on a single day during the 1991 Twins World Series parade. During the 1992 season, well over 100,000 people went through the doors of our store. Which, according to former Twins catcher Earl Battey, is "more than the Old Senators."

The Twins placed championship t-shirts in their windows in an unsuccessful attempt to lure our customers away. The 1987 playoffs marked the turn around for the business. The entire Twins season from April to September had netted us a total of $55,000. Our rent alone was over $60,000 per year. The public got behind our store from that point forward. Many people thought it was terrible that the Twins would attack such a small business. One woman came in looking for a Twins outfit for Halloween. I said, "I'm sorry, we are sold out of them, but where do you live?"

She informed me that she lived in Brooklyn Park and I recommended another store for her to shop. "I can't do that," she said. "My husband said that I could get the outfit only if I bought it from Ray Crump."

"Do I know your husband?" I inquired.

"No," she answered. "He saw what had happened to you on television and thought it was awful." Many people felt the same way, and that's when our business took off.

After the year, I returned triumphantly to my accountant. I said, "Well, I told you I would make money."

Schachtman said, "Well, you didn't know that they were going to have the World Series games and playoffs here."

"That's true," I said. "The other thing I didn't know is that I was going to be raided and it would help me so much."

People do not like to see the small guy get kicked, which is what happened to us. I have battled since day one that I've been in business and have fought a lot. The people around the Dome feel that they can monopolize the area. It's like they had a big pie. I came along and took a sliver of the pie, followed by a slice of the pie. That bothered them. They are so used to pushing people around and getting whatever they desired.

Bill Lester, the director of the Metrodome, summed up the belief of the stadium administration. In an article in the *Star Tribune* in 1992, he said that they are not in a big hurry to find places for people to spend their money before they get into the stadium. Thus, most of the areas near the Metrodome are parking lots.

Before I rented the building at 406-410 Chicago Avenue,

I drove down to the Metrodome. The NCAA was holding the regional basketball game in the stadium. There were five hundred people standing outside the locked gates, and I knew I was on to something. The fans had a strong survivalistic desire to escape the harsh winter, but lacked viable options. I hoped that the people would come into my building when it opened, warm up, and make a few purchases. My hopes were fulfilled.

When I first made the negotiations to rent the building, I only wanted or needed to rent 2000-3000 square feet. They wouldn't rent to me unless I took the entire floor, which was 13,500 square feet. I accepted this since I really didn't have a choice. I wanted the building. I saw its potential. I subleased part of my space to a local hospital for storage purposes. Later, business was very successful, and the hospital moved out of the back of the store. I knocked down walls to expand the store into formally unused storage areas.

When we eventually opened the store, we had an extremely low budget. We were trying to come up with a name for the business and decided upon "Dome Souvenirs." After talking about what we would have in the building, we decided that we should change the name to "Dome Souvenirs Plus." Thus, we could facilitate every additional point of interest that we added to the business.

At first, helmet boxes acted as counter tops, peg board was hung on the wall for displaying a few shirts, but we were open for business. The first day, the Milwaukee Brewers were playing across the street. We sold a $1.99 submarine sandwich to someone who wasn't even attending the game, and souvenirs sales were nonexistent.

The second day, I went outside to throw away some trash. Three boys entered the store and ran out with three Starter jackets. A loss of $120, my wife cried and was ready to quit. Scalpers were outside making more money than us, with no taxes or rent to pay.

In January of 1987, we decided to open The Original Baseball Hall of Fame Museum of Minnesota as a way to increase store traffic. The whole family contributed to make a room, and fill it with artifacts that I collected through my involvement with professional baseball. We lined the ground and hallways of our building with the old artificial turf purchased from the Metrodome. We wanted to give people the sensation of walking on the same turf as had been used and spat on by hundreds of baseball and football players.

People from around the world started coming to visit the free museum and store to see the eclectic display of baseball jerseys, bats, autograph balls and related memorabilia. Three days after we had taken the items out of our basement for placement in the museum, there was a terrible flood. We had four feet of water in our home, which would have ruined a large portion of the collection. Things must have been turning around.

To further promote the business, I had fliers being passed out before games and I made up signs to be posted on the telephone poles around the Metrodome. The signs read: "Free baseball museum, probably the only thing on Chicago Avenue that's free." Police officers came into our store when it was extremely busy and said they had received a complaint and ordered me to take the signs down.

"Bullshit!" was my reply.

The next day I went to the Minneapolis Police Department and met with Deputy Chief Leonard Brucciani. He checked on the complaint and found there was no call. Thus, the call hadn't been funneled through the standard police channels. It had to come from somewhere else. He believed that the officers were off-duty policemen working at the Metrodome, and they were sent over to harass us.

A man came into a store and said someone in a yellow golf cart was driving around taking down the signs off the poles. I went out to investigate. I found Neil Peterson, who was in charge of the Metrodome's parking, out pulling off the signs. He had gone as far as two blocks away from the stadium to remove the signs on company time. I never found out who had ordered him to tear down the signs. We try to keep a sense of humor about all of this. If we didn't we might need to seek professional help, because it does drive us crazy at times.

I decided to install a public address system on my building. The entire set up with two speakers and wires cost a total of $29.99. I would shout out information over the speakers to tell fans going to the game about the free museum and store. Soon after this, the Metropolitan Sports Commission held a meeting and decided to add their speaker system to the Metrodome. Their speaker system cost thousands upon thousands more.

Twice, I received tickets from the officers who worked in the Metrodome for our speakers being too loud. The ticket came from Captain Gary Hanies who was off-duty at the time. I later checked and there had been no formal complaint, thus Captain Hanies was sent over from the Dome. This was yet another form of harassment against our business.

I went to discuss the tickets with Minneapolis Mayor Don Fraser. I told him the whole story and he was confident that I would win a court battle against the violation. He said, "If

314

you go before the judge and tell him the same thing your telling me. I have to believe that you will get the charges dismissed."

Twice, we went to court to fight the tickets for violating the noise ordinance. Each time, we were let go without penalty. On one occasion, the judge said that "The Metrodome and the Minnesota Twins need to remember that they are no larger than the law." I was ordered to turn down the speakers, but the opposition wanted them to be removed.

After we added the museum to the store, I watched the various customers reactions. I'm generalizing, but I noticed the father and son would go into the museum while the mother sat and waited. I wanted to give people something to do if they didn't care for baseball very much. I took some pictures that I had in my home featuring me with famous celebrities. Throughout my life, I have always made a hobby of meeting people. I have photographs with people from Frank Sinatra to Bill Cosby to the Beatles to Mickey Mantle. We took these pictures and mounted them in the hallway. A new addition was founded, "The Hallway of Celebrities."

Next came "Elvis' Corner." I took various items I had collected from Elvis Presley and created a little shrine to him. There are tour jackets, autographed photographs, hankies, buttons, programs and other items. People have really enjoyed this section. Some anonymous people have left flowers and cards on the anniversary of his death and birthday.

The biggest event ever held at the Metrodome was Super Bowl XXVI on January 26, 1992. We did very well during Super Bowl week, but we could have done a lot better on the day of the game. The city was petrified of the possibility of having traffic near the Dome. Thus, they required all vehicles traveling near the stadium had to have a pass. This frightened thousands of people who wanted to be downtown for the excitement of the biggest sporting event of the year. The media all advised people to stay away, and the passes further cemented their fears. The much heralded ten days of Super Bowl hype was suppressed. People did stay away and it definitely had an impact on our business. We had ordered merchandise on a very conservative level with regard to other retailers in past Super Bowls. Yet, due to the streets being barricaded, we lost a lot of business. Instead of having orderly traffic flow, the area looked like a police state.

Despite the disappointing business aspect of the Super Bowl it was a very exciting time. The media from around the world often entered our store to create stories for their audiences back home involving souvenirs sales in the area. Muhammad Ali surprised everyone by stopping in the store on Super Bowl

Sunday. He posed for photographs, signed autographs, and did a magic trick, which displayed a flower in his previously empty hand, before departing.

Our sales have been helped a great deal due to the intense media coverage of our store. Whenever a major event happens at the Dome or to a local sports team, the local media contact us hoping to show Minnesotans the latest designs. For example, as soon as the Minnesota Vikings won the Central Division Championship in 1992, we sent out faxes that invited the press to show the new shirts. These "Fax Attacks" have been very advantageous for us, and the local media are glad that we are willing to work so close with them. Of course, we get a priceless amount of free advertising by appearing on television.

We have had a few very big sells that caught the media's eyes. The first one occurred right before Frank Viola was traded to the Mets in 1989. A short time before the transaction, we had a "Frank Viola Half Price Sale." The media jumped all over this and the next day, Frank was sent to New York. We did the same thing when Hershel Walker was having a rough time during his stint with the Minnesota Vikings. The team had mortgaged its future to obtain his services, but he fell far short of expectations. Thus, we dumped all the items that had his name or picture on just before he was released from the club. Selling players is similar to playing the stock market. You must be prepared to dump the commodity before the bottom drops out.

Sales representatives play a very important role in any business. Especially in our business of Championships, timing is very important. After the raid, we were informed that our orders would be delayed or screwed up in some way. Of course, we were unable to get a deposition from anyone, because they all didn't want to get involved.

Fortunately, some sales people have come through for us and we cannot thank them enough. A young woman from Rawlings called just to inform us we would get our order as planned. She said her company had no intention on listening to an outsider dictate whom they should sell to.

Steve Endquist was also very helpful in getting the shirts we needed for the Championships in 1987, 1991, and also the Super Bowl and Final Four. He was always there for us and even helped when our sales staff was overwhelmed. Dale May, from Salem Screenprinting, has also helped us receive quick service on merchandise. With the help of these dedicated people, we are able to get our products out to the consumer as quick as possible.

In early September during the Twins 1987 trip to the post season we came out with the "Domer Hanky." Our staff artist,

Roger Krafve, drew a picture of a man penetrating the Dome's roof reading a newspaper. He had to have created the design before September 15th, since he left the company for three months on that date and he drew the design before he left. We placed a large banner on the side of our building and sold quite a few of the hankies. During the first playoff game, the *Star Tribune* gave away thousands of their "Homer Hankies." This started a trend and the newspaper sold tons of these dollar squares of fabric. We sold only hundreds compared to their millions, but we had a significant part in the trend. Ever since that September, we have come out with hankies involving the various events in the Metrodome.

In August, 1991, we came out with another hanky. The caption read: "The Dome Boys are for Real." And they were. Yet, the Twins investigated this item. A couple of Twins employees came over and purchased two hankies, and brought them back to the Twins offices. Doug Grow, a sports columnist for the *Star Tribune*, said the Twins' lawyers were trying to find a way to sue us for copyright infringement. The Twins were coming out with a second "Homer Hanky," entitled, "The Magic Continues." I told Grow the story of us coming out with the original "Domer Hanky" in early September, 1987. The Twins never followed through with any kind of lawsuit, since they didn't have a case, but Grow vowed to write a story about their treatment of small business if they had followed through with their plan. The amusing thing about the entire "Homer Hanky" phenomenon involved the woman who created the *Star Tribune's* original design. The newspaper made a truckload of money from sales and she received a personalized license plate.

We have had these problems before with the Twins. I talked to Tony Oliva, and we decided to make up a couple "Tony O'" shirts. The shirts had Oliva's statistics, name, facsimile signature and photo on them. We made sure that the shirts did not contain the Twins name and/or logo on them. I made an agreement with Tony, in which I would give Tony a portion of each shirt sold. Again a Twins employee came into our establishment and this time, they purchased the Tony Oliva shirts. The Twins Director of Novelties, Matt Hoy, approached Oliva with the shirts. He said, "That guy across the street is selling shirts with your picture on them."

"I know, I gave him permission."

His face showed the stress of becoming angry. "Well, why did you do that?"

"Because, you wouldn't come out with a shirt with my picture on it." Matt Hoy walked away in a huff, and we continued to sell hundreds of the shirts. I was pleasantly surprised to see the two shirts they purchased from us on display at the Metrodome during the Twins' Fan Fest.

We had a big series in August, our best month, and we needed someone else to work the food counter since one of our regular employees couldn't work. We tried to handle the job Saturday night without the employee, but were overwhelmed. I told Carol, "There's no way I'm going home tonight without getting someone to help us for tomorrow."

I drove up the street and saw a clean-cut man riding a bicycle. I pulled over and asked if he knew anyone that wanted to work in a snack bar. He said, "I might want to. Where's it at."

"We have a snack bar by the Dome, and we need someone to work Sunday morning."

The man hopped off his bike. "Well, my brother-in-law is out of work and he would like the job. But, if he doesn't I'll promise you to be there for sure Sunday."

I gave him my home number and he biked down the street. He called me that night and guaranteed me that he would be there at nine a.m.

The next morning, the clock struck ten and no one showed up. I started to get worried, because I knew people would start to pile into the place. I walked down Chicago

Avenue. At the end of the road, there is a mission. I went inside and heard a man hollering. A preacher had a hand on Ron's shoulder and another on his head. He shouted, "Save Ron! Save Ron! Dear Lord, Save Ron!"

I waited outside the building until Ron came out. I walked over to him, "Do you need work?"

Ron answered, "Yes."

"Well," I said in desperation. "The Lord told me to come here and give you a job."

His eyes became very big. "Really? When did you want me to come and work?"

"The Lord said that he wanted you to come work for me right now."

We walked to the store and Ron said, "He sure picked a good time."

I looked at him and said, "Yes, he did."

Ron worked with us for a few months, and did a satisfactory job.

The business I built with the help of my family experienced remarkable growth. In fact, it appeared too good to be true. Sales increased every year, regardless of the success of the Twins and Vikings' seasons.

When the time came to renegotiate and extend our lease, we wanted another long-term lease for the building. Cowles Media was unwilling to give more than a one-year lease, since they "are not in the leasing business." We decided having a short lease would be better than relocation. Instead of a full year, we decided nine months would be more advantageous to our business. The original lease stated that we would have to vacate on March 31. By ending the lease after the Vikings season, December 31, we wouldn't have to pay six thousand dollars a month to be close to an empty stadium. We felt it was the best alternative for the business and Cowles Media company could realize how much money they were making on the property in the midst of a recession.

From October of 1992, we tried to work out an agreement for a long lease with Cowles Media. They never gave us any indication we couldn't continue our relationship. The building was over one hundred years old, but was in good shape. The boiler had been recently serviced and we were told by the technician that it would last at least another five years. Cowles Media claimed that it had to be replaced at a cost of $80,000. We decided to ask the boiler company about a replacement and were told that $20,000 was the maximum cost and the new unit would be more energy efficient. We tried to

323

offer our landlord a new heating system in exchange for a long-term lease and were told "That's an option."

We were told that the restrooms had to be made handicapped accessible, but they had always been accessible to the physically disabled. We should have realized that they hadn't bothered to check out the facilities.

We suggested that Cowles Media try to rent out the additional floors, but they weren't interested. There were many options for the building that they didn't even consider. The building was doomed and there was nothing we could do about it.

After all of this haranguing, Cowles Media did not see the property in the same way. They sent a letter to me, which stated their desire to evict the business and free museum. The eviction notice was stamped with the Santa Anonymous logo as though I would be in a generous mood upon its receipt. Until I received the letter, everything appeared to be well. The building would be slated for demolition to create an additional forty-eight parking spaces.

We fought very hard to change the plans of this corporation, since the decision was obviously illogical. We did the math and determined the impossibility of them making more money off parking than we paid in rent. The parking spaces they possessed were never sold out, thus there was no need for more. Even if they sold out every Twins, Vikings, and Gophers game, we still paid more in rent. I wouldn't go down without a fight. With my family's help, we organized "Save the Museum" petition drives. The local news stations covered the event like a funeral, and various newspapers carried the obituary. Hundreds of people sent letters and called the *Star Tribune* to protest their decision. In the end, the paper and Cowles Media were unswayed by the emotional outcry.

We determined that the *Star Tribune* was unable to see beyond newsprint and asphalt.

We didn't look at only one option through the protest, we searched and found another building. It took much negotiating, but we were fortunate to find a new home for Dome Souvenirs Plus and the Original Baseball Hall of Fame Museum of Minnesota.

The new building is much smaller than our first home, but it has potential. Across from Gate A at 910 South Third Street, it is the closest possible building to the Metrodome.

I lost a lot of sleep worrying about the re-zoning of the new location. We can thank the Minneapolis City Council for voting unanimously in our favor, including one absentee vote. I can honestly say we feel we are in business today because of the fax attack and offering a free museum to our fans.

After over $25,000 in renovations, the museum and business was open for the start of the 1993 baseball season.

We at least can look back and chuckle at the empty spaces among new asphalt where our old building used the stand, and we view the emptiness as a shrine. There is life and business after the demolition of a grand old building. With any luck, the new location will be as full of stories as the rest of my life has been.